OLDE
LONDON
Punishments

OLDE
LONDON
Punishments

Alan Brooke & David Brandon

The
History
Press

First published 2010

The History Press
The Mill, Brimscombe Port
Stroud, Gloucestershire, GL5 2QG
www.thehistorypress.co.uk

British Library Cataloguing in Publication Data.
A catalogue record for this book is available from the British Library.

ISBN 978 0 7524 5456 6

Typesetting and origination by The History Press
Printed in Great Britain

Contents

1

Changing Punishment Through the Centuries

London has a long history of criminal activity and an equally long history of brutal public punishments. Whippings, brandings, mutilations, transportation and public humiliation in the stocks and the pillory, all of which ended in the nineteenth century, existed for a range of offences. Before 1868 many of these were part of the public spectacle. These gruesome displays attracted huge crowds to the various sites of execution and torture where people would witness, or perhaps be entertained by, the grisly spectacle of the condemned going through the agonies of their proscribed ordeal. This section will look at the development of punishments in London (although these punishments were also implemented elsewhere).

In the seventh century, King Ethelbert I introduced what seems to have been the first written English penal system. Punishment was based on fines, with sliding scales of compensation for the victims of the crime. A person who was assaulted and lost an eye, for example, was entitled to 50s from the assailant, whereas a lost toe only rated 6d. Often the rate varied with the social status of the victim and assailant. This system was refined by the Danes who had a very complicated tariff of compensation which meant, quite literally, that every man had his price. The Crown also took a share of the fine and often of the assets of the offender – a stealth tax. An ingenious fund-raiser was the selling by the Crown of pardons – even in advance of any crime being committed. It was, in effect, a form of insurance on the part of those who thought that they might well offend in the future and wanted to take out precautions.

As far as the penal system was concerned, women did not count. Little is known about how this system worked out in practice. Perhaps it did not work very well, if only because fines evaded the question of the element of revenge which is so critical where punishment is concerned. In the tenth century, whipping and mutilation were introduced. Canute gained the throne in 1016 and his reign was noted for unprecedented social peace. Perhaps this was because offenders were liable to being scalped or having noses, ears or eyes removed. William the Conqueror was not prepared to put up with any nonsense and added removal of the testicles for certain offences, although he also abolished the death penalty. The right to inflict this had previously been shared between the Crown and the barons. Astutely, William, wary as ever of any potential rivals for power, concentrated the official infliction of punishment under the auspices of the Crown.

It was during William's reign that ecclesiastical courts were established to deal with offences against the Church while civil courts adjudicated on crimes against the people. Generally, the ecclesiastical courts levied less severe punishments and so better-off laymen who were literate started claiming that they were priests and demanding to be tried in the Church courts. This anomalous practice was known as 'claiming benefit of clergy' and clearly discriminated against the poor. Over the centuries, more and more people took advantage of this loophole. Even a total ignoramus who managed to memorise the first verse of the Fifty-First Psalm was entitled to claim clerical privilege. This became known as the 'Neck Verse' and went as follows: 'Have mercy upon me, O God, according to thy loving kindness: According to the multitude of thy tender mercies, blot out my transgressions'. Continuing abuse of this practice led to the creation in 1496 of offences which were 'non-clergyable'. This meant that anyone charged with an offence such as the killing of his lord, master or sovereign could not plead benefit. Soon afterwards, anyone who had been convicted of a clergyable offence was to be branded on the thumb so that they could not enjoy the privilege a second time. Then it became possible to pay a bribe which meant that a cold iron would be applied to offenders who had the money.

After William died, his son William II reintroduced the death penalty for poaching deer in the royal forests, and Henry I extended capital punishment. The belief was that only God knew whether a suspect was innocent or guilty and to help the Almighty make up his mind on such matters, trial by water or fire was devised. In the case of the latter, the theory was that the guilty would float and the innocent sink. In the case of fire, the accused had to hold a red-hot bar and if, three days later, his skin was not scarred he was deemed innocent. Less drastic was subjecting offenders to public ridicule as a deterrent. This practice was particularly applied to bakers of underweight loaves or brewers who over-watered their beer. Such a baker might be humiliated by being drawn around the town on a hurdle with an example of an offending loaf tied around his neck. His standing in the community – and his business – might be seriously damaged by this punishment. Sometimes the offending loaves would be made available for the crowd to pelt the dishonest baker. A brewer might be forced to drink as much of his substandard beer as he could swallow and then have the rest poured over him. More serious offences such as murder, treason, burglary and robbery carried the death sentence.

In 1154, Henry II came to the throne and embarked on an overhaul of the legal and penal system which involved ensuring that every county had a prison used to house those awaiting trial or sentencing. Other reforms included amputation of the right hand and right foot for robbery, murder and coining, rather than death.

It was in the thirteenth century that trial by jury was introduced. Corporal punishment involving the use of stocks for minor offences and the whipping post and the pillory became common. The idea of public humiliation can be seen in all these instruments. A new punishment was outlawry. The victim, his family and property, if any, lost all the protection of the law and thereafter they were friendless. In the early years they could be killed with impunity by any citizen. Those who harboured them or gave them succour could be punished. Several monarchs found outlawing highly profitable: it enabled them to sequester the property of the outlaws.

In 1241, hanging, drawing and quartering was introduced for those guilty of treason. The victim was drawn through the streets to the place of execution – initially they were dragged along the road but this was found to be inconvenient because it injured or sometimes killed them prematurely. For that reason it became normal to convey them on a horse-drawn hurdle. They were then hanged until almost on the point of expiry, whereupon they were cut open and eviscerated, their entrails often being burnt in front of them. On occasion, they would be castrated. Lastly, they were dismembered.

Temple Bar, where body parts were once displayed, now stands near St Paul's Cathedral.

Painful death by crushing.

Often their limbs and especially their heads, treated with preservative, were put on display in some prominent place. The gates to London Bridge were one favourite location. It used to be the practice to take a family walk on a Sunday and go have a look at how the heads were doing. From 1684, Temple Bar was another place where the heads and various body parts of traitors might be found. Spyglasses could be hired for closer scrutiny of the grisly remains posted up there.

Convicted felons and their families forfeited all their property. This could leave a spouse and children in poverty. It was reasoned that if an accused person refused to plead, they could not be tried: if there was no plea, how could there be a trial? This greatly irked the authorities and in 1272 measures were taken to persuade suspects to lodge a plea. Initially they were placed in irons and stretched out, immobilised, on the floor and half-starved for a few days. This usually had the desired effect, but for the more stubborn ones worse horrors could follow. A torture known as *peine forte and dure* (strong and hard pain) involved pressing them by placing heavy metal weights on their chests and bellies. Those that were not killed usually pleaded quickly enough rather than put up with the excruciating agony. Pressing was not regarded as a torture or a punishment, but merely as a method of persuasion. Those who had been pressed then had to undergo a trial and, if found guilty, the likelihood of being hanged.

Hanging was the most common method of execution but those of noble blood were entitled to the 'privilege' of decapitation with sword or axe.

Heresy began to be a serious issue in the fourteenth century. Heretics were viewed as dangerous people who dared to question the political and religious status quo. In criticising the power structure of medieval society, they were regarded by the authorities as offending God, who had ordained how society should be organised, and the reigning monarch, who was God's representative on Earth.

The reign of King Henry VIII (1509-1547) inaugurated many legal changes. He permitted Sunday executions and introduced boiling to death. He also made a substantial number of other offences non-clergyable. These included piracy, rape and highway robbery. Beggars and wandering robbers increased in numbers, especially after the monasteries were dissolved, and were dealt with by being whipped. In official circles, poverty and criminality became virtually synonymous. Vagrants were often branded with a letter 'V' after their first conviction and from 1572 had a hole bored in the gristle of the ear. Houses of correction were built to punish vagrants and to put the able-bodied 'idle' to work. Whipping posts became familiar items of street furniture.

Whipping became one of England's most commonly used forms of punishment, used not only against vagrants but as a standard sentence for petty larceny, the theft of goods worth less than 1s. In 1589, appropriateness was the criterion for decreeing the

Being whipped through the streets was a common punishment.

Site of William Hunter's Anatomy Theatre, Windmill Street, Piccadilly.

loss of ears for uttering seditious words and of the right hand for producing seditious writings. Such punishment, of course, left the offender with visible evidence of guilt and dishonour. People who absented themselves from church services were liable to have their ears removed, showing that they had chosen not to hear the Lord's word.

During Henry's thirty-eight-year reign it was estimated that around 70,000 people were executed in England. The rationale was that tough measures were needed to deal with those whose activities offended God (and the King). The effect was to provide a legal and penal framework within which the rising middle-class enjoyed the social stability thought essential for the country's economic development. Henry, incidentally, inaugurated the practice whereby barber-surgeons were given the bodies of executed felons for research and demonstration purposes. From 1540, they were provided with four cadavers annually. This number increased in the eighteenth century amid considerable controversy. Public dissection of dead felons was used as an aggravated punishment.

Queen Elizabeth I (r.1558-1603) was one of the monarchs who made use of banishment from her realm. Although this might seem humane by comparison with capital punishment, the effect on the recipient was not unlike outlawing, made worse by the fact that the victim was likely to find himself penniless, powerless and probably friendless in a foreign country.

During the period of the Tudor monarchs, heresy and treason tended to conflate and were considered to be of the utmost seriousness. Most heretics were bunt at the stake. This appalling method of execution usually involved the victim being smeared with pitch or tar, tied to a post and then surrounded by a combustible material such as brushwood. The executioner then used a noose to render the prisoner unconscious before the flames reached him or her. Sometimes this did not work and the prisoner died in unspeakable agony. Britain's last recorded burning at the stake occurred on 18 March 1789 when a woman was put to death in this fashion outside Newgate Prison. Her crime was coining.

Despite the increasing severity of the penal code in Tudor times, the general impression was that crime was an increasing threat. In the somewhat hysterical climate that resulted, nobody seems to have been surprised when a senior legal figure seriously suggested pulling out the tongues of convicted criminals.

The concept of punishment continued to embrace both physical pain and public humiliation. Petty offenders might be placed in the stocks or the pillory, whipped or fined, or two or more of these punishments. The pillory was extremely painful because the offender was held by the neck and wrists, causing agonising cramps. Sometimes, to aggravate the punishment, the offender had his ears nailed to the hinged wooden board in which his neck was placed. This prevented him ducking when a hostile crowd pelted him with all manner of filth or, if they really disliked him, with stones. Sometimes offenders were fatally injured by such missiles. If their feet did not reach the platform on which they were standing, they risked slow throttling.

Occasionally, if the authorities felt particularly vindictive, they might further aggravate the punishment. In 1630 a Dr Leighton who wrote a book lampooning royalty, the peerage and the upper echelons of the Church of England, was whipped severely and had one ear cut off before being pilloried. He also had the septum of his nose split and was branded with the letters 'SS', indicating that he had stirred up sedition.

During the Interregnum (1649-1660), the judgmental and joyless heavy hand of Puritanism descended on the English and on their favourite activities and pastimes. 'Incontinence' now became punishable. This word was used in the sexual sense and made fornication a misdemeanour and adultery a felony. Abusing the sanctity of the Lord's Day also became a misdemeanour and uttering profanities and gambling with cards became punishable. With the Restoration, there was a huge communal sigh of relief but severe punishments continued to be imposed for a wide range of offences. The State seemed determined to keep the whip-hand – literally – over a populace which was seen as becoming increasingly fractious and insubordinate, most of all in London, .

Nowhere did the perceived threat from crime seem as serious as in London. The capital offered unique opportunities to the criminally inclined. Its population was large and growing rapidly because of inward migration. The result was the creation of a rootless and volatile population, many of whom were unskilled and very much at the mercy of economic downturns and slumps. While some people migrated to London willingly, thinking they could make new and better lives for themselves there, in reality very few did. Economic and social changes were forcing people off the land. Possessing few loyalties or moral precepts, many inward migrants naturally turned to crime, especially when times were hard. London offered propitious conditions for criminal activity because of its concentrations of very evident wealth, its anonymity and the feebleness of its law-enforcing agencies. Probably the greatest incentive to criminal activity is a low arrest and conviction rate. Often those who arrived in the metropolis were young and single, and concern was expressed about the prevalence of youth crime. Additionally, London attracted disbanded soldiers and sailors, those who would now be described as 'illegal immigrants' – perhaps foreign sailors who had jumped ship. Refugees, wandering Jews, misfits, desperadoes; London had always been a social and ethnic melting pot, now more than ever. London developed sophisticated criminal and underworld networks.

A sixteenth-century English visitor to London gives a colourful assessment of what he saw:

> …If you come to London, pass through it quickly. Each race brings its own vices and customs to the city. No-one lives in it without falling into some sort of crime. Every quarter of it abounds with grave obscenities. Whatever evil or malicious thing that can be found in any part of the world, you will find it in that one city. Actors, jesters, smooth-skinned lads, Moors, flatterers, pretty boys, effeminates, pederasts, singing and dancing girls, quacks, belly-dancers, sorceresses, extortioners, night-wanderers, magicians, mimes, beggars, buffoons: all this tribe fill the houses. Therefore if you do not want to dwell with evildoers do not live in London.

Parliament created a very large increase in the list of capital offences during the eighteenth and nineteenth centuries in an attempt to counter what was perceived as a serious increase in the level of crime. However, penal policy was by no means straightforward. Of course there were always those kinds of people around who thought hanging was too humane and that felons should, for example, be broken on the wheel instead. On paper there was a ferociously deterrent penal system. For example, what became known as the 'Waltham Black Act' of 1722 was aimed ostensibly at poachers but was used as a Trojan horse to introduce the death penalty for a host of other supposedly 'rural' crimes. In 1688 there were about fifty capital offences. Between 1660 and 1819 no fewer than 187 additional offences came to carry a capital sentence. These included cutting hop-bines, setting fire to coal mines, defacing Westminster Bridge, concealing the death of an illegitimate child, damaging a fish pond, stealing a shroud from a grave and bigamy.

Much has been written about Britain's 'Bloody Code', with horror stories of how children of twelve or less were despatched to the gallows for shoplifting, or how felons were transported for offences that now seem trivial. This suggests a brutally retributive penal system that was the desperate response of the authorities to levels of crime that were getting out of hand. The reality was more complex because, in practice, the criminal law was also characterised by elements of pragmatism and humanity. In the eighteenth and early nineteenth centuries, the courts increasingly imposed non-capital punishments on convicted felons. These might involve detention with hard labour or transportation to the American and later the Australian colonies. Between 1827 and 1830, 451 people were convicted of capital offences in London but only fifty-five of them were actually hanged.

Juries frequently practised what was sometimes called 'pious perjury'. They often mitigated the severity of the law when prisoners were charged with capital offences. For example, where a prisoner was charged with theft, the jury might undervalue the articles stolen. This reduced the crime from a felony to a misdemeanour, which attracted a lesser punishment. Judges on their own initiative sometimes dismissed cases and reprieves were by no means uncommon. Felons were often sentenced to transportation rather than hanging. A number of women avoided the death penalty by pleading 'benefit of belly' because they were pregnant. This allowed them a reprieve until the baby was born and in practice usually mean that they were pardoned. Women in Newgate awaiting trial or execution often bribed the warders to allow men to visit them for the purposes of sex. The outcome, they hoped, would be pregnancy.

The courts exercised an unpredictable, capricious mixture of terror, humanity and clemency which added powerfully to their mystique. The elaborate rituals whereby bewigged judges in ermine-tipped, scarlet robes donned the black cap when death sentences were solemnly pronounced emphasised the majesty of the law and tended to overawe those who offended against it. However, flexibility in how the law was applied could mean inconsistency. The court's decision might be unclear until the very last minute, greatly heightening the tension. On occasions there were 'general' reprieves in celebration of particularly auspicious public events and these could result in even hardened recidivists getting off scot-free.

What was the rationale that underpinned the penal system in the period up to 1800? Three main principles can be identified. One was the concept of deterrence. It was believed that the very public ceremonies involving the condemned prisoner's last journey to the place of execution, the rituals around the gallows and the felon's subsequent agonising death were effective deterrents. Retribution was another facet. The suffering attached to the punishment should be proportional to the heinousness of the crime. The third principle was that the offender, even one guilty of a minor crime, had shown his disregard, even his contempt, for the values around which society operated. Therefore it was entirely right and proper that punishment should involve shame and humiliation in public.

The ultimate punishment for City of London and Middlesex criminals up to 1783 was public execution at Tyburn. This provided unequivocal evidence of the State's legal monopoly of violence. Since the majority of those hanged had offended against laws protecting property, each hanging was intended to send out a clear message that property and the law should be respected. Few people possessed any significant wealth and so the use of this deterrent was evidence of the conflict of interests between the rich and powerful and the poor and disenfranchised. However, was hanging really such a deterrent when pickpockets employed their skills to profitable effect in the crowd massed around the gallows?

From the eighteenth century significant changes were taking place: the reform of criminal law, prisons, and punishments. By 1800 the vast majority of those convicted

Bow Street Magistrates Court in Covent Garden.

of a felony were transported to Australia or incarcerated for periods from several weeks to years, often in hulks, floating prison ships moored in the Thames. There was a growing concern, especially from those in positions of authority, that the public hanging of people was not having the desired effect of deterring people from committing crimes.

The thriving market in tabloid-style journalism was quick to recognise the insatiable appetite for sensation and titillation. It fed that appetite with descriptions of lurid crimes and the gruesome punishment of offenders.

The eighteenth century also saw the beginning of serious criticism of the penal system. Henry Fielding, the Westminster and Middlesex JP and co-founder, with his brother Sir John, of the Bow Street Runners, deplored the exhibitionist nature of public hangings and the way in which they either made serious miscreants into swaggering, popular heroes or placed in the limelight the pathetic behaviour and lack of dignity of those unable to hide their terror. He argued that 'the executions of criminals serve a purpose diametrically opposed to that for which they were designed; and tend to inspire the vulgar with a contempt for the gallows rather than a fear of it'. In practice, most offences went undetected because of the lack of an effective police force and only small numbers of those convicted of felony were hanged. The criminal could therefore go about his activities knowing that he had a good chance of evading arrest and conviction, let alone a premature death on the scaffold.

What system of law enforcement and punishment there was depended upon constables who were expected to keep the peace. There were also night watchmen, or 'Watch', who patrolled the streets, and thief-takers who received rewards for arresting and convicting criminals. Night watchmen originated in the reign of Charles II (1660-1685) hence their nickname, 'Charleys'. Thief-takers were often knowledgeable about what was going on in the criminal fraternity and this, combined with the system of reward, often led to corruption.

Those convicted of forgery and coining were very rarely pardoned, but the frequency with which these crimes continued to be committed strongly suggests that hanging was not an effective deterrent. The question of how to deal with rising levels of crime elicited proposals that varied from increasing the number of capital offences and greater use of corporal punishment to the employment of alternatives such as custodial sentences involving reform and rehabilitation. Enlightenment thinkers, especially in Europe, argued that crime was a problem with economic and social causes that could not be solved merely by creating ever more severe punishment.

Reform was in the air and by the time that Victoria came to the throne in 1837, the number of hanging offences had come down from well over 200 to just fifteen. These offences included murder, arson, rioting, robbery with violence, piracy, wrecking, serious sexual crimes and the theft of government money or securities. Two decades later the number of capital offences had been reduced to just four. The number of hangings in London was falling significantly and a long period of almost uninterrupted economic growth, combined with the presence of the new Metropolitan Police, led to a considerably enhanced sense of security. In 1834, one of London's executioners had been laid off because there was insufficient work for him. Branding had ended in 1829, gibbeting was abolished in 1834 and the pillory in 1837. Public hangings continued until 1868. Transportation ended in the same year.

London's population grew at a phenomenal rate. By the end of the nineteenth century it had grown to over seven million. Migration had contributed greatly to this expansion. As London expanded in size and population during the eighteenth and nineteenth centuries the issue of maintaining law and order became a matter of public concern. The reliance upon part-time officials proved inadequate in dealing with law-enforcement. Conditions in London became intolerable and begged for an effective and organised system of policing. Until 1829 arrests depended upon the victims apprehending a criminal and then contacting a police constable, hence the regular hue and cry of 'Murder!' or 'Stop thief!'.

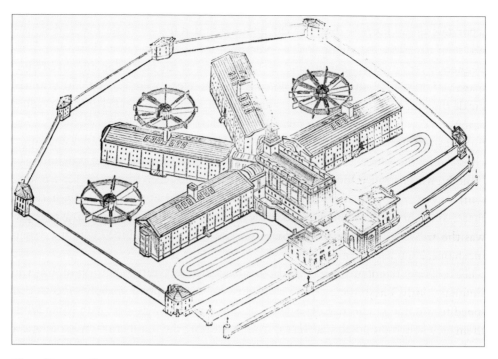

Plan of Pentonville Prison.

Reform may indeed have been in the air, but as always it was an uneven process. The prisons of London continued to be dire establishments – cold, insanitary places with regimes that often sought only to punish the prisoner, break his personality and dehumanise him rather than to encourage him towards reform and rehabilitation. Contemporary wisdom favoured the idea of putting prisoners to work in solitary confinement. New prisons such as Pentonville were built to put this concept into practice. Each block had single cells on several floors radiating like the spokes of a wheel. When attending chapel or taking exercise, prisoners were masked and prevented, at least in theory, from communicating with each other. This deprivation of human contact and the hours of solitary confinement frequently drove prisoners insane. Highly imperfect though such prisons were, the use of such places to punish the offender gradually won support as preferable to transportation overseas.

Contemporary thinking favoured the infliction of soul-destroying labour on prisoners undergoing penal servitude. An example was supervised 'shot-drill'. Heavy iron balls of shot were picked up and passed around a circle of prisoners, but only after each man had placed the shot on the floor and stooped to lift it up before giving it to the man at his side who in turn put it down, and so on. The rationale was to destroy each prisoner's 'excess energy'. 1¼ hours of this in the open on a hot day turned even the strongest man into a weakened and quaking mass of human misery. Less physically demanding but mind-numbingly boring was oakum picking. This involved separating the individual fibres of rope cables discarded from sailing ships. The oakum was then put to use in caulking the planks and decks in wooden ships. The ropes were frequently filthy with congealed tar and other substances and in unpicking the rope, masses of floating tarry fibres were released and were of course easily inhaled by the luckless convicts. It is no wonder that many prisoners mutilated themselves or tried to commit suicide – anything that would secure an escape, even a temporary one, from this enforced and pointless employment.

Idleness among the inmates was seen as something to avoid at all costs. It was thought, usually by those members of the upper classes who had never done a day's work in their lives, to erode morale and morality. Not for nothing did they intone that 'the Devil makes work for idle hands'. The *beau ideal* of this school of thought was the treadmill invented by William Cubitt (1785-1861). William was a noted mechanical and civil engineer. It was a devilishly ingenious device in the form of a wheel 16ft in circumference and wide enough to accommodate twenty-four prisoners simultaneously. They supported themselves on a handrail and 'walked' at sufficient speed to rotate the massive heavy wheel twice a minute. Care was taken to partition them off from their fellows as they underwent their sessions on the wheel. It was a studied exercise in pointlessness intended to break their spirit and to punish them for being prisoners. It was physically extremely demanding. Each prisoner was required

A treadmill at Brixton Prison.

to complete fifteen sessions of fifteen minutes each daily on this contraption. This was roughly equivalent to climbing a mountain over 7,000 feet high – and this on prison rations! Nothing tangible, not even milled grain, was ever produced by the treadmill. Some prisoners were literally 'broken on the wheel' in mind and body. For the toughest, it simply bred hatred. An expensive and simplified device was invented in 1840. The 'Crank' could be operated by one man who turned a long handle attached to heavy weights. It was back-breaking and demoralising, precisely as it was intended to be.

Wormwood Scrubs Prison was opened in 1874 and completed in 1890. It was based, even at this late date, on the already discredited 'separate system', although it broke with normal practice in consisting of several parallel blocks of buildings. Much of the construction work was done by convicts. From the start it contained some of Britain's most dangerous prisoners.

In 1877 the Prison Act brought every English prison under the jurisdiction of the Home Secretary. They were now paid for by central government out of taxes and immediate responsibility for their operations was placed under a group of commissioners. One intention was to introduce uniform standards and regimes throughout the prison service, but this proved impossible to achieve in the short-term. The treadmill and crank continued to extort their toll of human misery for many more years. Another Prison Act was passed in 1898 which introduced the idea of remission of sentence for good behaviour. The crank and treadmill were abolished and excessive corporal punishment was ended, at least in theory. While official thinking may have been that prisons should prepare their inmates for making a better fist of things once they were released, individual governors had much autonomy and many of them continued to do things as they had always been done. It took a long time for the idea of reform, education and rehabilitation to become accepted practice. In reality, retribution and revenge have never really left the penal agenda.

2

The Prisons of London

This chapter explains the role of the prison in the eighteenth century, and provides a brief outline of the history of some of London's major places of confinement.

The concept of the prison as a place of long-term confinement for people convicted of serious offences did not really exist before the eighteenth century. Periods of imprisonment were usually brief – often a year or less – and were imposed for a curiously eclectic range of offences. Among those who were consigned to prison were those convicted of offences including perjury, combining against employers, manslaughter and commercial fraud. Offences regarded as felonies and therefore of a more serious nature carried the death penalty but in practice the courts exercised considerable discretion in applying capital sentences when they were extended to a widening range of offences in the eighteenth century. The 'Bloody Code' looks rigid and vindictive, but its application was extremely flexible. The arbitrary nature of sentencing probably increased the awfulness of the law because a court's decision was so difficult to predict. Transportation gave the penal system a welcome alternative to capital punishment. In the late 1760s, as many as 75 per cent of those convicted for felony at the Old Bailey were transported. Transportation was a very convenient, 'out of sight, out of mind' sanction leavened by a hint of clemency.

In the middle of the eighteenth century, three major institutions of confinement can be identified in London: debtors' prisons, jails and the houses of correction commonly known as bridewells. In London, debtors were confined particularly in Ludgate, King's Bench, the Fleet and the Marshalsea. Debtors were consigned to these institutions until such time as they were able to discharge their debts or Parliament let them off the hook by passing an act declaring them 'insolvent'. The regime under which these prisoners lived seems curious to modern opinion because the inmates were maintained at their creditors' expense. Debtors could live with their families, could enjoy visits from friends and business contacts and did not have to undertake the various tasks that came the way of the ordinary prisoners. In fact, they were virtually able to run their businesses from the prison or to leave it daily to work and earn wages. Those able to come up with the

The Viaduct Tavern which stands opposite to the site of Newgate Prison. It was built shortly after the last public execution in 1868.

necessary financial means could rent privileged accommodation and in some cases they even sublet some of it. If they could discharge their debts, they obtained their freedom.

The whole system was corrupt and mercenary. Prisons were let out to contractors whose major concern was to maximise their profits. They would provide almost any service in return for cash. Debtors were frequently the kind of people who did not allow mere financial embarrassment to stand in the way of their enjoyment of life and its varied, often expensive, pleasures to the full. The keepers of the Fleet and King's Bench were prepared to allow debtors to live outside their respective prisons if a suitable financial arrangement could be reached. Debtors were not treated as felons but were often a disruptive element, especially on those occasions when they were confined alongside criminals. Many of them were irritatingly querulous and acted as 'barrack-room lawyers', inciting discontent and insubordination among the other inmates.

The second category of institution was the local jail controlled by a county or a borough. Few of these were large establishments, and Newgate was by far the largest of them with more than 250 inmates in 1750. These prisons contained debtors, people awaiting trial, some prisoners serving short custodial sentences and those waiting to be transported. The rules said that the different classes of prisoner should be kept apart but in practice, largely because these prisons were understaffed, the inmates mingled and developed a regime whereby most goods and services could be obtained in exchange for cash. These jails were run for profit by contractors who cut financial corners wherever they could. The actual keepers found many ways to add to their meagre wages by further scrimping for those prisoners who could not buy favours and selling favours of all sorts to those who could. Many prisoners only survived on the support of friends and relatives.

The bridewells or houses of correction were sometimes a separate part of a major jail or buildings entirely on their own, and they were more numerous than the other types of prison. Their ostensible purpose was to tackle the problem of vagrancy by housing 'sturdy vagabonds' and other ne'er-do-wells, the able-bodied who were not prepared to work. By combining elements of punishment with set tasks for the prisoners, the house of correction was the only type of prison at this time whose regime contained at least some sense of trying to reform its inmates. It was hoped that the experience would persuade them to value the work ethic. In some places the local industries in which there was a lot of outwork relied very heavily on the labour provided by the house of correction. The work involved was unskilled and monotonous. It is stretching

Bridewell in the eighteenth century.

the imagination to believe that inmates who, for example, spent their time picking feathers as stuffing for mattresses, found this an encouraging introduction to the world of work. In their turn, the businesses concerned faced the low productivity inherent with forced labour. The regimes within the various houses of correction varied widely. All were dirty and pest-ridden, but an inmate who underwent a brief stay in the Clerkenwell House of Correction in 1757 made it clear that many of its prisoners spent the time lounging around gaming, drinking and fornicating.

In the eighteenth century, London contained the largest prisons and a disproportionate share of the country's total prison population.

Newgate

Newgate is the prison whose name most readily springs to mind when mention is made of the 'Tyburn Tree'. Unfortunately the early records of Newgate's use as a prison are sparse but it is likely that the first gaol with that name was located over the Newgate entrance to the City itself; it was certainly in existence in 1189 because it is mentioned in a Pipe Roll of that year as a royal prison. John Stow (1525-1605) in his seminal *Survey of London*, published in 1598, mentions that in 1218 Henry III told the Sheriffs of London to ensure that the gaol at Newgate was kept in good order. In 1241, London Jews were threatened with imprisonment in Newgate unless they paid a fine of 20,000 marks during a wave of anti-Semitic hysteria. In its early years Newgate seems to have played the role of high-security prison for political and other high-profile prisoners, not only from London but also from the provinces, and others who could not be housed in county gaols. It was its role as a royal or state prison that led to the opening of a small gaol designed for many of London's petty offenders in the nearby Ludgate.

Newgate was the prison for both the City of London and the County of Middlesex and it had already acquired an evil reputation by the early fourteenth century. In 1334 an official enquiry into conditions in Newgate revealed that even prisoners on minor charges were incarcerated in deep dungeons which they shared with hardened recidivists and all manner of other woebegone inmates, some of whom were not necessarily criminals but were simply unable to cope with life. They were subjected to systematic brutality from the keepers and many depended for their existence on charity. Although under the overall jurisdiction of the city sheriffs, Newgate was in effect privatised and its day-to-day management was let out to contractors who saw it as a source of income by which they could enrich themselves over and above the contractual financial arrangements they had made with the sheriffs. All sorts of services were available to those prisoners who had deep pockets. It was a living hell for those who did not.

Newgate suffered attack and considerable damage from the insurgents during the uprising in 1381 under Wat Tyler. In 1419 the keeper and sixty-four of his charges perished in an attack of the plague. 'Gaol fever', a form of typhus, was ever-present as

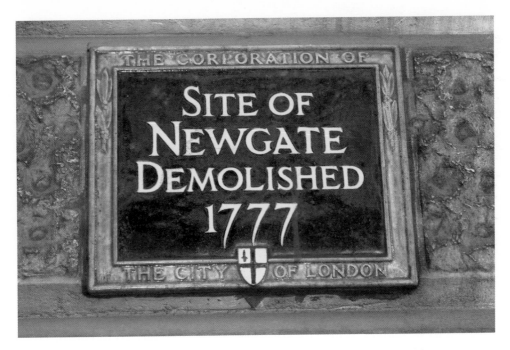

Plaque outside the site of old Newgate Prison.

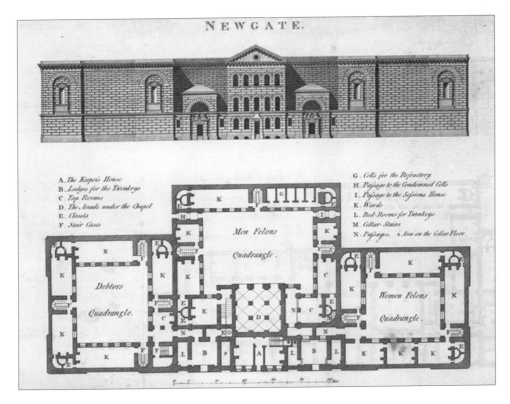

Plan of Newgate Prison.

the rats and lice which spread the *Rickettsia* pathogens found ideal conditions in the foetid, insanitary and overcrowded surroundings. In 1423 a sizeable enlargement and refurbishment took place and this was undertaken using money pledged by the late, very wealthy Sir Richard Whittington. For a while Newgate became ironically known as 'Whittington's Palace' and was palatial in size compared to the previous premises. It had a dining hall and separate accommodation for different classes of offenders. It was also more secure but it swiftly deteriorated because the infamous old system of leasing it for profit continued, even though from 1440 it had supposedly been more carefully scrutinised by the sheriffs.

A practice which had been operating for many years was that of 'garnish', whereby the keepers or turnkeys found ways of extracting money from new arrivals for even the barest necessities such as candles and soap. Many rackets were practised to extort money from prisoners. One example was 'ironing the prisoners'. Most prisoners were placed in heavy iron shackles when they were admitted. These were removed before departure but not before fees were extorted by the keepers for both fixing the shackles and taking them off. It was probably no coincidence that the fees were very similar in amount to the bond that the keeper was expected to pay for every prisoner who escaped.

By the 1690s the office of keeper could be bought and sold. In such a situation it was perhaps inevitable that the fabric of Newgate should deteriorate: repairs ate into the keepers' profits. This only exacerbated the overcrowding problem as the miserable inmates were packed into those parts of the building that were still useable. In turn the overcrowding encouraged the spread of the gaol fever and other contagious diseases. The bulk of prisoners had no duties to attend to all day and simply loafed about causing trouble, usually for the weaker of their brethren. Some of the less feckless prisoners managed to make items which could be sold outside the prison, but often had difficulties in pocketing the proceeds because of the presence within the prison of a ubiquitous and omniscient mafia. They would run a range of rackets, often in conjunction with the keepers themselves and involving systematic extortion and violence. The prison subculture was very deep-rooted and mock trials were not uncommon. They would ridicule the official process of the law and bore considerable similarity to the long-standing tradition of charivari, or rough justice, perpetrated by the community on those whose behaviour it particularly disapproved of.

Browbeaten and bullied by staff and fellow-prisoners alike, those who had no money or could not stand up for themselves might be consigned to the remotest, coldest and darkest parts of the prison without any heating, bedding and with the barest minimum of food. However, anything could be bought in a prison like Newgate. Drink flowed freely and banquets were enjoyed by the well-to-do. The well-off might also be able to pay to have their spouses or partners living with them. Prostitutes conducted lucrative business in prisons. Some prisoners had their pets with them, a practice which cannot have helped the chronic overcrowding or the general ambience. A pamphlet appeared in 1717 explaining that access to the superior lodgings in Newgate required a down payment of 20 guineas and an ongoing rent of 11s a week. The services of a cleaner could be had for 1s a week and a whore for the night cost 12d. In fact, the regime inside the prison was little different from that on the outside. The one thing that money could not usually buy was freedom.

The City authorities must bear much of the blame for the abuses which took place in Newgate: their aim seems to have been one of systematic neglect while trying to avoid drawing attention. In 1628 a structural survey was undertaken which described Newgate as a 'ruin' desperately in need of repair, the cost being estimated at £500. Newgate was damaged severely in the Great Fire of 1666 but was rebuilt with rather fine decorative embellishments on the outside (which contrasted greatly with what rapidly became the noisome conditions which had to be endured by its inmates). Nothing was done to improve the supply of fresh water or to make provision for effective ventilation. The irony of equipping Newgate with a splendid façade with prominent statues symbolising 'Peace', 'Security', 'Plenty' and 'Liberty' was not lost on the satirists of the day.

In 1665 the plague had struck Newgate with lethal effect. Fear of the plague is entirely understandable, and led to the temporary suspension of court sessions. Unfortunately, this may have caused even more deaths, as prisoners who might have been acquitted were kept confined with other prisoners in conditions where fatalities from plague were bound to be high. In fact, the conditions inside Newgate in the early eighteenth century were so pestilential that many of the condemned felons sent there before being taken to be hanged at Tyburn got no further, succumbing to gaol fever and other epidemic scourges. The nadir was probably reached in 1750 when Newgate was more than usually overcrowded, and inmates who appeared in the nearby Old Bailey seemed to bring an almost tangible contagion with them. In May, more than sixty people attending the Old Bailey died as gaol fever raged indiscriminately through prisoners, judges, jury and anyone else in attendance. Such a disaster led to prisoners from Newgate being soused in vinegar as a disinfectant before they appeared in court and to the practice, still extant, whereby judges on certain occasions carry nosegays with them as they enter court. Immediate steps to counter the foulness of Newgate's atmosphere included building an open exercise yard and a windmill on the roof as a primitive air extraction device. Such was the smell emanating from Newgate, particularly in hot weather, that passers-by would cross the street to avoid the stench and keep their noses covered!

The prison had many notable inmates over the centuries. These included Anne Askew, the English Protestant martyr who was racked in Newgate and burnt at Smithfield, the highwayman Claude Duval in 1670 and Daniel Defoe in 1702 and 1703. The darling of the London crowd, Jack Sheppard, the burglar, highwayman and escapologist, was in and out on several occasions in 1723 and 1724 – and the hated Jonathan Wild was incarcerated in 1725. With the exception of Defoe, when the others finally left Newgate, it was to undertake their last journey. In most cases this was to Tyburn. Innumerable other wretches 'went west' from Newgate.

The hated Jonathan Wild displayed on a 'Tyburn Ticket' for his execution.

Jack Sheppard in Newgate Prison.

An entertaining feature of life in Newgate was the presence of the chaplain or ordinary whose ostensible job was to cater for the spiritual welfare of the inmates. The services this man offered cut little ice with most of Newgate's residents (except perhaps when they were *in extremis*). Routine services were frequently a noisy shambles as the ordinary struggled to make his voice heard above the uncouth and irreverent hubbub of his captive audience. For all that the ordinary had an important role to play in the carnivalesque atmosphere that was expected in Newgate on the day before a felon was taken off to Tyburn to be hanged. This involved the condemned prisoner being taken to the prison chapel where he was subjected to an extremely lengthy tirade from the ordinary about the need to expiate his sins before his awful imminent death. Partly dependent on the notoriety of the prisoner, the chapel would be crowded with members of the public who had paid good money to see how the condemned bore up to this very stressful time. On occasions a spirited prisoner would sit and shout insults and obscenities at the ordinary – and this of course was exactly the kind of entertainment the audience had paid to see.

Despite the fact that the ordinary was generally held in low esteem and his pastoral efforts were so fruitless, when a vacancy occurred there was no shortage of applicants for the post. It was not usually the cream of the clerical profession that were attracted to the Newgate ordinary's job: in fact, some who obtained the job were inhumane brutes who were only there because of the opportunities for peculation. These centred on the highly profitable writing and selling of broadsheets – usually known as the Ordinary's Accounts – which claimed to contain the condemned prisoner's last confessions and utterances. Sometimes the ordinary would browbeat a frightened prisoner into a confession that he might then embellish with gory and salacious detail. This would then be printed and would sell among the teeming crowds around Newgate, along the route to Tyburn and by the scaffold. If a suitable basis for the 'confession' was not forthcoming from the prisoner, most ordinaries were not above simply inventing one. In his book *The London Hanged*, Peter Linebaugh summed up the ordinary's role with customary felicity: 'Between the justices and the hangman, one of the most coveted positions and one of the most loathed, stood the Ordinary of Newgate whose unenviable task it was to justify the decisions of the former and to lend Christian sanction to the dark work of the latter'.

The conditions in Newgate continued to attract criticism even after the City bought back the right to appoint the keeper in 1734. All seemed to agree that desperate action was needed as the deaths continued and the fabric crumbled further. However, the authorities seemed incapable of reaching any accord on exactly what should be done and how it should be paid for. In 1770 another rebuilding was started which included knocking down that part of the old Newgate gateway to the City that had for so long been incorporated in the fabric of the prison. The new building was scarcely complete when it was again the butt of the mob's rage, this time in the Gordon Riots of 1780. Much of it was demolished in a frenzied and sustained attack during which the insurgents managed to release most of the inmates. The prison was rebuilt to a grand design as it had been just before the riots by the highly thought-of architect

The gallows at Newgate Prison.

The Gordon Riots of 1780 destroyed Newgate Prison.

George Dance the Younger. Dance was the Clerk of the City Works and in turn was influenced in his design by the Italian architect Piranesi. It reopened in 1783, in which year executions ended at Tyburn and were transferred to the area just outside Newgate. Ironically, one of its first inmates was the very same Lord George Gordon whose crazed rabble-rousing had fomented the riots of 1780 named after him. He died in Newgate in 1793. He hosted lavish dinners and dances while serving his time and entertained so many guests in his cell that it was frequently a case of standing room only.

It is clear that the authorities had not really seriously considered how the space outside Newgate would cope with the massive crowds attracted to especially piquant hangings. Their neglect had tragic effects in 1807. In that year an angry crowd of about 40,000 gathered to view the hanging of John Holloway and Owen Haggerty who had been convicted of murder but were generally believed to be innocent. In the intense press, someone fell. Others tripped and also tumbled down. Panic broke out and twenty-eight people were crushed to death.

The prison's rebuilding did not terminate the appalling conditions and vociferous criticisms continued to be heard throughout the rest of its life, most of all about the overcrowding and the unsanitary conditions. In 1811 the House of Commons established a committee to enquire into conditions in prisons. Newgate was supposed to hold 300 inmates, but on the day that members of the committee visited it, the number was no less than 900 felons and 300 debtors. One outcome of this visit was the opening of a debtors' prison in Whitecross Street in 1815 which helped to relieve the overcrowding.

From 1852, Newgate was used only to house prisoners awaiting trial or execution. Hangings ceased outside Newgate in 1868. It went out of regular use as a prison after the Home Office took over control in 1877. Demolition started in 1902 and when this was completed, in 1904, the Central Criminal Court was built on the site.

Newgate seems to have exercised a macabre fascination for Charles Dickens and it features particularly in *Barnaby Rudge* and also *Oliver Twist* and *Great Expectations*. The prison also appears in Thackeray's novel *Henry Esmond* and Harrison Ainsworth's *Jack Sheppard*.

Coldbath Fields

Coldbath Fields was located in Clerkenwell, close to a natural spring, and was built in the 1790s, quickly becoming notorious for the severity of its regime. It was this notoriety which encouraged Samuel Taylor Coleridge (1772-1834) to pen the following lines:

As he went through Cold-Bath Fields he saw
A solitary cell,
And the Devil was pleased, for it gave him a hint
For improving his prisons in Hell.

Coldbath Fields gained more literary distinction when Samuel Butler in his semi-autobiographical novel *The Way of All Flesh*, published posthumously in 1903, has his character Ernest Pontifex confined there. The inmates of Coldbath Fields at one time numbered as many as 1,400. It closed in 1877.

Not far away was the Clerkenwell House of Detention, built in 1615. This had an eventful history. It housed numerous Catholic priests, was attacked by London apprentices in 1668 and briefly housed Jack Sheppard and his lady-friend Edgeworth Bess before they made a cunning escape. Tobias Smollett (1721-1771) lodged his character Humphrey Clinker from the eponymous novel in Coldbath Fields, often known as the 'New Prison'. The prison was attacked during the Gordon Riots of the 1780s but underwent rebuilding and extensions over the next sixty years. In 1867 a Fenian trying to rescue some compatriots from the house of detention blew a huge hole in the wall, demolishing a row of artisans' dwellings opposite and killing six people and injuring fifty others. He did not manage, however, to extract the prisoners. Although it was rebuilt, the house of detention closed in 1877.

Bridewell

Bridewell came to give its name generically to houses of correction and gaols. The original building was a royal palace on the banks of the Fleet. It was completed in 1520 for Henry VIII, and took its name from a nearby well dedicated to St Bride or Brigid. Its years of glory were brief. In 1522 Charles V, the Holy Roman Emperor, was entertained to brilliant pageants and banquets by Henry at Bridewell Palace. On 30 November 1529 Henry dined there with Catherine of Aragon, this probably being the last time she saw her husband. In 1553, however, the palace became a temporary lodging place for the indigent and a prison for petty offenders, later adding a hospital and workhouse function. Much of the fabric was destroyed in the Great Fire but was quickly rebuilt, after which the building's prime purpose was as a prison. Bridewell was closed in 1855.

'The Clink'

On the south bank of the Thames in the Southwark area there were many penal establishments, but one of the best known was 'The Clink'. The word 'Clink' is now an apt generic nickname for any prison: it so easily provokes thoughts of keys turning in locks and body irons being rattled by helpless and despairing prisoners. The original 'Clink' was located on land controlled by the Bishops of Winchester. These bishops took a pragmatic view of the real world with all its flaws. Obviously, they decided, sin was an inescapable feature of the human condition – and therefore they might as well cash in on it. For that reason, the bishops allowed a large number of brothels, bawdy-houses and other disreputable establishments to operate on their land in Southwark, all the while maintaining their right to police and otherwise control them. These enterprises provided a consistent and generous income for hundreds of

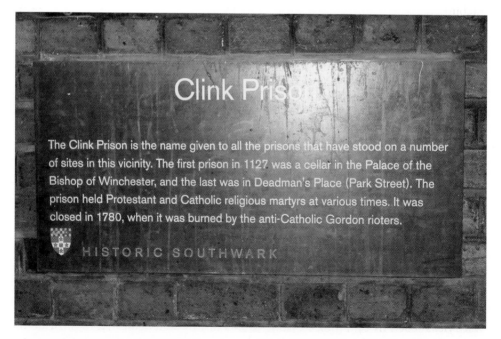

Sign outside the Clink Prison, Bankside.

The Clink Prison Museum.

years, and some of the bishops themselves were not above enjoying the services of the prostitutes (who were often referred to as 'Winchester Geese'). Those who used these establishments in Southwark sometimes broke the rules, and the bishops therefore needed a facility in which offenders could cool off and ruminate at leisure on the wages of sin. This, then, was the origin of 'The Clink'.

It was in use as early as 1161. In 1381 it was attacked during the Peasants' Revolt, and again in 1450 during Cade's Rebellion. On both occasions the attackers took a great delight in releasing the inmates. 'The Clink' was noted for housing debtors and famous inmates including the Protestant Martyrs John Bradford and Bishop Hooper in 1555, as well as the Catholic recusants of the sixteenth and also seventeenth century. 'The Clink' went into a long decline after it was removed from the jurisdiction of the bishops. It burnt down in the Gordon Riots in 1780. It was not rebuilt.

The Marshalsea

Close by in the Borough was the Marshalsea. Dating from the fourteenth century, it was originally used as a state prison and was second only in importance in that respect to the Tower. When rebels attacked London, it almost seems to have been *de rigeur* to attack one or more prisons. The Marshalsea was no exception, being attacked by Wat Tyler's rebels in 1381 and again by Jack Cade's followers in 1450. Notorious for its awful conditions, there was a great riot and mass breakout at the Marshalsea in

Plaque to the Marshalsea Prison, off Borough High Street, Southwark.

1504. Those involved were ruthlessly hunted down and many of them hanged. This seems particularly vindictive given the fact that the building was a most ramshackle establishment from which escape must have been relatively simple. It is known that prisoners frequently bribed the keepers to be allowed to enjoy the pleasures that went with an *exeat*.

In 1557 this prison housed Gratwick, one of the Protestant martyrs who, after his trial, was burned to death in St George's Fields. When Elizabeth succeeded her sister Mary on the throne, one of her first actions was to incarcerate Bonner, the last Catholic Bishop of London, in the Marshalsea, where he died some years later. In 1601 one Christopher Brooke took up residence for the unusual crime of giving a young lady by the name of Anne More in marriage to the poet John Donne without the knowledge – and therefore the consent – of her father.

Conditions in the Marshalsea were atrocious. In 1728 it was reported that the inmates were suffering unduly because of the frugality and cruelty of the keeper, William Acton, who used the post to supplement his main income as a butcher. Many prisoners died of neglect and starvation. A row broke out but although there were calls for Acton to be charged with murder, he served only a short prison term and little was done to improve the regime. In 1738 an anonymous pamphlet called *Hell in Epitome* described the Marshalsea as, 'An old pile most dreadful to the view, dismal as wormwood or repenting rue'.

Remains of the Marshalsea Prison wall.

As with a number of other prisons, the site of the Marshalsea was changed, in this case on a couple of occasions, to locations close by. This was done because the old buildings seem literally to have been falling down. In the final reincarnation of the Marshalsea, which opened in 1811, Charles Dickens's father was briefly imprisoned for debt in 1824 and this experience was incorporated by the novelist into *The Pickwick Papers* and *Little Dorrit*. The Marshalsea was closed in 1842, by which time it contained only three prisoners. It was amalgamated with the King's Bench and the Fleet.

King's Bench

The third of Southwark's major prisons was the King's Bench. This owes its curious name to the gaols attached to the court of King's Bench, which travelled around the country from town to town.

It was certainly in existence during Wat Tyler's Rebellion in 1381, and by 1554 it included John Bradford among its inmates. Bradford had been condemned to death in the Church of St Saviours, now Southwark Cathedral, and was shortly after burned at the stake at Smithfield for his faith. Other Catholic and Protestant martyrs spent time within this prison in the sixteenth and seventeenth centuries before, in most cases, going to their deaths elsewhere. During the Commonwealth, with an eye to contemporary political correctness, the prison was known as 'the Upper Bench',

'King's Bench Prison', by Augustus Pugin and Thomas Rowlandson (*c.* 1808-11).

but it later reverted to its original name. In 1670 Richard Baxter resided there as a result of his stand against the Act of Uniformity which established new regulations for the Church of England after the monarchy had been restored. He seems quite to have valued, even enjoyed, his sojourn in the King's Bench. He was accompanied by his wife and, as he explains in his *Autobiography*, 'We kept house as contentedly as at home, though in a narrower room, and I had the sight of more of my friends in a day than I had at home in half a year'. A particularly unusual prisoner was the King of Corsica, who spent several years in the King's Bench after 1752, attempting to work off his debts.

In 1758 the King's Bench moved from the east side of Borough High Street to a new and much larger site only a short distance away in St George's Fields. Its internal arrangements seem to have been extremely austere but contemporary records make mention of drink and facilities for playing various competitive games. Probably these were only available to the well-off prisoners. Certainly it was possible for wealthy prisoners to buy a licence which gave them the right to visit the taverns, brothels and other places of entertainment within three square miles of the prison.

Among its early prisoners was Tobias Smollett, a writer who in 1760 was deemed guilty of libel for an article about Admiral Knowles which appeared in the *Critical Review*. He wrote his novel *Sir Lancelot Greaves* while he was in the King's Bench. John Wilkes (1727-1797) was housed in The King's Bench between 1768 and 1770. He was already immensely popular with the London crowd for his general irreverence to those in positions of power and his identification with the cause of 'liberty', but he had been forced to flee abroad when he had been found guilty of obscene libel for his poem

Essay on Women. On his return, his popularity was confirmed when he was elected in 1767 as MP for Middlesex amidst scenes of huge popular jubilation. However, he decided it was expedient to surrender instead, whereupon he was committed to the King's Bench. Large and supportive crowds accompanied him as he was escorted to Southwark. William Combe (1741-1823) was a prisoner for many years and it was in the King's Bench that he wrote *Dr Syntax's Three Tours*, which were scathing satires on contemporary travel books. Whatever income he received from these was insufficient to pay off his debts.

Another inmate consigned on several occasions to the King's Bench for debt was also one of the prison's most colourful occupants: the artist Benjamin Robert Haydon (1786-1846). Attempting to make a living as a portrait and landscape painter, he did not allow lack of talent to stop him producing large numbers of paintings of biblical and historical subjects, all of exceptionally poor quality. In spite of his practical shortcomings as an artist, Haydon was a very fine teacher of art history and a trenchant art critic, one of whose main targets was the Royal Academy. This obviously did not endear him to the art establishment and as a result he lost much of his credibility and struggled to sell his works. His literary efforts received greater recognition but the most successful of these, his *Autobiography* and *Journals*, only received major plaudits after he had died. Haydon spent several periods in the King's Bench for debt and committed suicide later. Charles Dickens gives the King's Bench a mention in *David Copperfield*: Mr Micawber was confined there.

The burial ground in the perimeter of Millbank Prison.

The King's Bench had been largely destroyed in the Gordon Riots of 1780 and its replacement soon became known for the superior accommodation it offered to wealthy inmates and the squalid conditions with which the poorer prisoners were forced to put up. Those who were prepared to pay for the privilege could actually take lodgings close to the prison, but there is some evidence that this licence was abused – to the extent that some prisoners actually resided overseas! In 1842 its name was changed to the Queen's Bench and it took over large numbers of debtors previously housed in the Fleet and Marshalsea prisons. It later became a military prison and was finally demolished in 1880.

Millbank

Millbank Prison was intended to be a model. Built at Millbank, Pimlico, it was opened in 1816 and eventually closed in 1890. In the prison's early years sentences of five to ten years were offered as an alternative to transportation, but it soon ceased to have a penitentiary function and became a holding centre for those awaiting transportation. It was designed by William Williams in 1812 in accordance with the principles laid down by reformer and philosopher Jeremy Bentham.

Morpeth Arms, Millbank, where the wardens of Millbank Prison drank.

One of the few remains of
Millbank Prison.

In the *Handbook of London* (1850) it was described as a mass of brickwork equal to a fortress. The external walls form an irregular octagon and enclose upwards of sixteen acres of land. Its ground-plan resembles a wheel, the governor's house occupying a circle in the centre from which radiate six piles of building, terminating externally in towers. The ground on which it stands is raised but little above the river, and was at one time considered unhealthy.

Millbank received its first prisoners in 1816 and stood on the lonely and marshy riverside linking Westminster to Chelsea. Charles Dickens described the area in *David Copperfield* (1849) as 'a melancholy waste... A sluggish ditch deposited its mud at the prison walls. Coarse grass and rank weeds straggled over all the marshy land'. Not surprisingly, many prisoners suffered from malaria. Nonetheless, Millbank Penitentiary was hailed as the greatest prison in Europe and held as a model for others to follow.

So complex were the three miles of cold, gloomy passages that the turnkeys invented a code of chalked directions to stop them from getting lost. It beggars belief that anyone could escape from this warren of tunnels. When transportation came to an end in 1868 the prison fell into disrepair and disrepute, despite its earlier promise, and was demolished in 1891. The prisoners were transferred to the newly built Wormwood Scrubs Prison.

The Fleet

The Fleet Prison was first mentioned in 1197 and was London's earliest purpose-built prison. It also served as a royal citadel, along with Baynards Castle and The Tower, from which the early Norman monarchs could browbeat their unwilling new subjects in the teeming streets of the City.

It seems to have been built on the most ill-favoured site of any of London's prisons. It stood on the east side of the Fleet River where it debouched into the Thames among a number of small, muddy and odoriferous islands that acted at that time both as a defensive moat and a barrier to escape. In dry summers the Fleet became almost stagnant. It was a convenient receptacle into which all those who lived and worked along its banks despatched their rubbish and effluents of every description. Its neighbourhood was considered to be especially obnoxious in a city already noted for the diversity and extreme repulsiveness of the stenches it produced. From 1343 things became even worse for the inmates of the Fleet Prison. In this year the butchers of nearby Newgate Street were given permission to use the Fleet to dispose of the unwanted items from their trade. A small tributary called the Faggeswell Brook already made its way into the Fleet after being used as a dumping ground for the slaughterhouses of Smithfield Meat Market. This stream brought much blood and offal with it and meant that when the Fleet was flowing sluggishly in hot summers, the area around the prison exuded a variety of rank odours dominated by the stench of festering animal refuse. In turn this provided the optimum conditions for all kinds of disease-bearing pathogens, which meant that the Fleet was probably the most pestilential of all of London's early prisons. It was said jokingly that a man might walk across the surface of the Fleet River where it passed the prison, so blocked was it by the foul and festering detritus.

The Fleet, being a royal prison, was used to detain those who owed money to the Crown, had in various ways displayed their contempt for his courts or who just generally got on the King's nerves. Royal it may have been, but the Fleet was like London's other prisons in that its running was put out to private contractors who were every bit as venal in their management of royal prisons as they were with those they ran on behalf of other authorities. In the case of the Fleet, a family called the Levelands managed to keep the management of the prison and its profits in their clutches for over 400 years. As one would expect under a regime run for profit, the Fleet allowed those with money to enjoy the best facilities available compatible with custodial confinement. The first prison on the site had suffered serious structural decay and was rebuilt in the reign of Edward III (1327-1377). Readers will not be surprised

'Fleet Prison' by Rudolph Ackermann, 1808.

to hear that the Fleet was destroyed by Wat Tyler's rebels in 1381. It was quickly rebuilt.

Over the centuries, the Fleet housed a number of distinguished prisoners, most particularly in the Tudor and Stuart periods. Among them was Henry Howard, Earl of Surrey (1517-1547), a noted writer of sonnets who was held on a charge of treason and later executed. Thomas Nashe (1567-1601) wrote a satirical comedy, *The Isle of Dogs*, which offended the authorities and led to him serving his time in the Fleet. John Donne, who died in 1631, was a prominent poet and later Dean of St Paul's who was imprisoned for marrying without his father-in-law's consent. James Howell, who died in 1666, was a writer and pamphleteer imprisoned from 1643 to 1651 for being a Royalist. The dramatist William Wycherley (1641-1715), meanwhile, was placed in the Fleet to work off his insolvency but was released on the orders of James II who (quite wrongly) thought that a character in one of Wycherley's plays was meant to portray him in a very flattering light. Few prisons can ever have housed such a galaxy of literary talent.

The Fleet was razed to the ground in the Great Fire of London and rebuilt on the same site. In 1691 a debtor called Moses Pitt revealed in his *Cry of the Oppressed* that on entry to the prison he had to part with £2 4s 6d to the keeper for the privilege of

Depiction of a Fleet Marriage.

Gambling on blood sports such as cock fighting was common, particularly in pubs.

being put in better quality accommodation even though the legitimate fee was a mere 4*d*. Other illegal fees were extorted from him until his money ran out – whereupon he was transferred to a dismal and stygian dungeon where he slept on the cold floor with twenty-seven companions, all 'so lowsie that as they either walked or sat down, you might have pick'd lice off from their outward garments'.

One common practice associated with the Fleet was that of improvised weddings. Previously, couples wanting to marry speedily and clandestinely had made use of the service available in the chapel in the White Tower within the Tower of London. When this ended, unscrupulous parsons transferred the business to the Fleet and its surrounding streets as they constituted a liberty with certain immunities from laws applied nationally. Touts patrolled the district seeking out couples who wanted a quick, no-questions-asked completion of the nuptials. Others sometimes travelled long distances in order to make use of the service. Probably the most corrupt aspect of this highly lucrative operation was the practice of entrapping sailors who came ashore after long voyages with money in their pockets, intent on obtaining drink and sex. They would be plied with drink and then supplied with a woman. While they were in their cups, marriage might suddenly seem like a good idea and they would part with large sums in order to pay for the necessary formalities. The reality of marriage, however, might not look so tantalising in the cold light of day... On one occasion as many as 173 weddings were performed in a day. This insidious practice was ended in 1753.

In the seventeenth century the Fleet was an especially dirty and corrupt prison. An enquiry in the early 1720s showed that the then keeper, Thomas Bambridge, made full use of every opportunity for abusing his position – including the rather unusual service of taking money to allow people to escape. To assist this he even had a door specially made for the purpose. He was promptly dismissed and new rules were brought in to apply to future keepers and their operations. John Howard, the prison reformer, visited the Fleet in 1774 and found it 'crowded with women and children, being riotous and dirty' and altogether poorly-managed. Once again it was burned during the Gordon Riots, but only after one of the rioters had rather politely informed the authorities that they should expect an attack. It was rebuilt and became notorious for the blatant abuses of authority enjoyed by the wealthier inmates.

However, no other prison seems to have equalled the Fleet for providing the facilities that allowed one of its inmates, Robert Mackay, to win the world rackets championship in 1820! An official inquiry into the management of the Fleet had taken place in 1819, which revealed that many women and children were sharing the prison accommodation with the inmates, prostitutes were plying their trade without hindrance, gambling for high stakes was rife and beers, wines and spirits were freely available. The report based on the inquiry was a very mild one which made few recommendations beyond suggesting that the prison's tap-room and coffee shop should be closed during divine service on Sundays. The Fleet features in *The Pickwick Papers* by Charles Dickens. The prison closed in 1842, by which time one of its last inmates had been immured there for no less than twenty-eight years. It was demolished in 1844.

The Tower

The final prison to be considered is the Tower of London. This is arguably the most famous castle in the world and has a long and extremely complex history. Here only the briefest of accounts of its role as a prison from early times until the early nineteenth century will be attempted. Leaving aside debates as to whether the site was fortified in Roman times, it is to William the Conqueror that the Tower owes its origin. He built it as an eloquent expression of his power and to impress upon the people of London the fact that Norman rule was there to stay. While William was busily establishing his domination it is likely that he would have imprisoned rebellious elements in the Tower, but the first record of a specific prisoner is that of Ranulf Flambard, Bishop of Durham, who fell foul of the Conqueror's successor, William II. The conditions of his imprisonment do not seem to have been particularly rigorous and he took advantage of this when he got his guards drunk and made his escape by means of a rope that had been smuggled in to him. He performed this daring exploit on 2 February 1106.

Traitors Gate, Tower of London.

The execution of Guy Fawkes at Westminster.

It was made all the more remarkable in that he is supposed to have insisted on taking his crosier with him as he escaped.

Dominating the site is that uncompromising, even brutal piece of military architecture known as the White Tower, the building of which started about 1078. In the 1240s, the English King of the time, Henry III, was engaged on one of the apparently endless wars with the Welsh. Prisoners had been taken and housed in the White Tower, one of whom, named Gruffydd, tried to escape in 1244 by the time-honoured means of knotting sheets together to make a rope. The improvised rope broke and Gruffydd fell to his death. Later in the same century, during a wave of anti-Semitism, the entire Jewish community of the Cheapside area (which was within in the liberty of the Tower and therefore under the jurisdiction of the Constable of the Tower) had to be taken inside for its own safety. Unfortunately, the Jews were an easily identified minority who also suffered gross persecution under the reign of Edward I. Edward incarcerated 600 Jews, mostly in the White Tower, on trumped-up charges of coin-clipping. Many simply starved to death in the stinking dungeons. In 1303 it is likely that the sub-prior of Westminster Abbey and several of his monks were confined while helping the authorities with their inquiries into an audacious robbery of the royal treasury. At the very end of the century, John Balliol, King of Scotland, (1249-1313), was lodged in the White Tower after his ignominious defeat by Edward I at the Battle of Stracathro in 1296; he enjoyed the relative luxury of leaving the Tower and being handed over to the custody of the Pope. Housed under far better conditions of confinement was King John II of France. He had been captured at the Battle of Poitiers in 1356 and spent three years of pampered luxury in the White Tower surrounded by servants and enjoying all the good things of life (except liberty) while the necessary money was raised to secure his release. In 1415 Prince Charles of Orleans, father of King Louis XII of France, was captured at the Battle of Agincourt and he languished in the White Tower for twelve years while an enormous ransom for his release was accumulated. He spent much of his time composing poetry.

In 1554 Sir Thomas Wyatt, leader of an abortive Protestant uprising against Mary, was housed briefly in the White Tower with some of his followers before being executed. Guy Fawkes was housed in the dungeons in 1605 while he staunchly withstood the attentions of his torturers and inquisitors and fed them a stream of false information. He was placed on the rack which eventually broke his will and he made a confession; however, he did not provide much of the information his tormentors really wanted. In 1671 Colonel Blood was imprisoned in the White Tower for the audacious crime of stealing the Crown Jewels. Amazingly, he was eventually rewarded for his enterprise with a lucrative government post in Ireland. Talk about cronyism!

The Tower of London is an extraordinarily complex set of buildings that have accumulated over time with additions, alterations and demolitions being made according to the needs of the era. Most of its towers have contained prisoners in the past. Two that are still in existence take their names from the family names of their best-known inmates: the Beauchamp and Devereux Towers. The Tower was widely regarded as virtually impregnable and therefore other, less fortified parts of the complex were used to house prisoners from time to time. An example is the Lieutenant's House close to the Bell Tower in the south-west part of the Tower. Here that tragic footnote to Tudor history, the cats-paw of manipulative and ambitious schemers, Lady Jane Grey, was lodged in 1554. She watched her husband Lord Guildford Dudley being taken away for execution at Tower Hill and saw his body brought back in a cart for burial shortly afterwards. Before he had made this short trip, he had whiled away the dismal hours by carving Jane's name in his cell. The carving can be seen to this day. Lady Jane made the same journey herself a few days later. An extremely illustrious prisoner a month or two later was the future Queen Elizabeth. Her half-sister Queen Mary (1553-1558) saw plots everywhere. She was no mean plotter herself. She had Elizabeth confined in the Bell Tower for a few months while under suspicion of plotting against her but the conditions under which she was kept were a good deal less onerous than those of many of the other poor wretches who were housed elsewhere in the Tower's precincts.

Henry VIII was the last monarch to use the Tower as a royal residence and once the facilities he used when staying there were redundant, additional space became available for its ongoing role as a prison. This space was to be particularly well-used while the Tudor and Stuart monarchs were on the throne. Politics and religion came together

John Fisher, a Catholic martyr executed by Henry VIII. Fisher's head was displayed on London Bridge.

at this time in an insidious and internecine symbiosis. Large numbers of prelates of both Protestant and Roman Catholic faiths – as well as laymen not prepared to abjure their religious beliefs – found themselves housed in the Tower for treason. Many were tortured. Those who were Catholics were frequently hanged, drawn and quartered, while Protestant martyrs were usually burned at the stake. The story of these turbulent years has often been told: suffice to say that at one time or other celebrities such as Thomas More, John Fisher, Thomas Cranmer, Nicholas Ridley, Hugh Latimer and William Laud were housed in the Bloody Tower, and that many Jesuits reluctantly made the acquaintance of the Salt Tower in the south-eastern corner of the precincts. Doubtless many other martyrs whose names have long been forgotten were also imprisoned in the Tower and died there for their faith.

Sir Walter Raleigh (1552–1618) was a long-term resident of the Tower. His life bears eloquent witness to the capriciousness of royal favour. In legend he is supposed to have gallantly taken off his cloak and placed it over a puddle so that Queen Elizabeth could keep her feet and long dress and undergarments dry. This courteous gesture, it is alleged, greatly flattered the Queen, but it seems to have cut little ice with her some years later when she had Raleigh placed in the Tower, admittedly under fairly lax conditions, for seducing one Bessy Throckmorton, one of the her maids of honour.

Judge George Jeffrey, the 'Hanging Judge'.

Eventually, breathing a sigh of relief, he was released – only to find himself back in the Tower in 1603, charged with plotting against King James I, the result of the machinations of the many enemies he had made over the years. He was condemned to death but then reprieved and placed under what was effectively house-arrest. This respite lasted for fourteen years, during which he wrote his *History of the World*. He then managed to obtain his release on the basis of leading an expedition in search of gold in South America; the freedom he obtained as a result of this mission proved short-lived, however, because the venture was conspicuously unsuccessful. On his return he was placed back in the Tower, and shortly afterwards taken to Westminster where he was executed.

The Tower continued to house prisoners for a further 300 years. A few of the most notable only will be mentioned. Escape from the Tower's brooding precincts was uncommon, but one who managed it was Sir William Seymour, who had been imprisoned by James I for his marriage to Arabella Stuart, a pretender to the English throne. In 1611 he succeeded in getting away from the Tower dressed in a carter's smock, with a wig on his head and sitting on a wagonload of faggots. Arabella, however, died in the Tower after several years of imprisonment. Other prisoners included John

Felton, who assassinated the Duke of Buckingham to huge public acclaim in 1628, and Edward Somerset, the Royalist Marquis of Worcester. It is said that one day, having nothing much to do, he took to watching a kettle boil and in a sudden flash of intuitive genius became the first person to realise the expansive force of steam and its potential as a source of power.

The wretched Duke of Monmouth resided very briefly in the Bell Tower before being executed on Tower Hill in 1685. With ironic justice, Judge Jeffreys followed Monmouth into confinement in the Tower where he died in 1688. In 1760 the egregious Earl Ferrers briefly resided in the Middle Tower before being executed for murdering one of his servants. Internment in the Tower was by no means always the prelude to execution. For example, in 1794 two radicals, John Thirlwall and Thomas Hardy, members of the London Corresponding Society, spent four months in the Tower; they stayed in quarters which Thirlwall described as 'large, airy and pleasant'. Presumably it all depended on what one was used to. Most of those who made the acquaintance of the cells and dungeons of the Tower would have used less complementary words to describe their surroundings.

Compters

Finally, brief mention should also be made of the Compters. These were under the control of London's sheriffs and were used to house petty offenders and debtors whose conditions of accommodation and the facilities they enjoyed varied, as did those of the inmates of the prisons, dependent on the depth of their pockets. These compters were not purpose-built and involved the adaptation of existing buildings. The gateway to the Poultry Compter, for example, was through a row of shops and houses. Other compters in the City of London included those in Bread Street, Wood Street and Giltspur Street.

3

The Hulks

The idea of sending undesirables to another country can be traced back to Elizabethan times when, in 1598, it was enacted that 'incorrigible rogues' who refused to live within the law might be banished to distant parts. Throughout the seventeenth-century Britain sent prisoners to America, notably to Virginia and Maryland, and many English, Scottish and Irish political and religious prisoners were sent to Barbados and Jamaica in the West Indies. Official sanction came with the Transportation Act of 1718, a measure prompted by the familiar public concern of a perceived growth in crime. Between 1718 and 1775, more than 30,000 convicts were transported across the Atlantic. However, this ceased when the American War of Independence started in the mid-1770s.

Britain needed to find an alternative system or destination urgently as prisons were already overcrowded and their condition a scandal. In something of a knee-jerk reaction, it was decided to house prisoners in old revamped fighting ships. The Hulks Act represented a fundamental break with the past and also contributed to the creation of a convict system very different to that of North America. These 'hulks' were moored on the River Thames at Woolwich and Deptford, as well as in other places such as Chatham, Plymouth and Portsmouth. The hulks were often unsanitary and overcrowded. When the first hulks were moored on the Thames at Woolwich it was intended to be a short-term measure. They continued for a further eighty years (1776-1857); the decision to send convicts to Australia came in 1786 and continued until 1868, and over 160,000 convicts were despatched 'Down Under'.

With regard to the hulks, the government from the start exercised a general supervision but their everyday operation was in the hands of contractors who tendered for the job, intending it to be a profitable business. It was soon discovered that far from being a cheap expedient, convict labour in the hulks was an expensive one because issues of security meant that the prisoners actually worked shorter hours than free labourers and, as is inevitable with forced labour, they did as little as they could possibly get away with. With the hulks being moored close to land and the work carried out by convicts ashore there

Illustration of an old hulk at Deptford.

was always a possibility that they would make a break for freedom. Effective security was expensive. In Charles Dickens' *Great Expectations*, his famous character Abel Magwich escapes from a hulk in the River Medway, in north Kent.

Some of the hulks were based close to each other on the south bank of the River Thames at Woolwich and Deptford, downstream from London. They housed only male prisoners, many of whom suffered from hernias owing to the physically demanding nature of the work they had to do. John Howard, the prison reformer, reported that of 632 prisoners admitted to one of them, *Justitia,* between August 1776 and March 1778, 176 (or 28 per cent) of them had died!

The hulks became full to bursting point and were notorious for their living conditions. Of all the places of confinement used in Britain, they were the probably the most demoralising. They were filthy, insanitary and overcrowded for much of the time. For example, records for the hulk *Surprize,* moored at Cove, near Cork, in 1834 show that there were 747 bowel infections; 1240 cases of 'the itch'; 392 of 'the cough'; 560 of 'feverish cold' and 284 'herpetic eruptions'.

Hardened criminals lived cheek-by-jowl with bemused and terrified first-time offenders – among whom were children, some not yet in their teens. Bullying, violence and abuse were rife. In 1847 it was revealed that an elderly man had been given thirty-six lashes of the cat o' nine tails for being just five minutes late for the early morning muster.

In the nineteenth century, those sentenced to transportation almost always found themselves temporarily housed in a hulk while awaiting a convict ship. A few weeks in a hulk were not an effective preparation for the hazards of a journey of several months to Australia, let alone for what might be awaiting the convicts when they got there. In some cases, prisoners supposedly awaiting transportation were 'temporarily' accommodated in hulks but remained in them until the expiry of their sentences.

The hulks were grim places for all concerned, and understandably those with the opportunity to do so tried to find a little light relief. In 1854 an official enquiry into incidents aboard the hulk *Victoria* at Portsmouth culminated in the court-martial of Lieutenant Charles Knight of the Royal Marines. It was alleged that on the night of the 17 September he brought two 'improper' women on board and proceeded to act 'improperly', plying both with large quantities of alcohol and possibly taking sexual liberties.

There were other disciplinary problems associated with the hulks. A letter from John Henry Capper, Superintendent of Hulks, dated 17 July 1832, raises the perennial issue of how to prevent the presence of hardened criminals 'polluting' other novice offenders. Capper writes:

> The great influx of youthful offenders matured in crime, who are daily received on board the Hulks from the several Gaols in Great Britain, make it advisable that a considerable number of Convicts should be sent to the Australian or other settlements during the present year; as it appears, judging from the report of their characters that, if discharged from any place of confinement in this country at the expiration of their sentences, there is but little hope of their pursuing an honest course of life.

The hulks were to remain in use as prisons and as temporary accommodation for those awaiting transportation for many more years. With squalor, disease, overcrowding, corruption and immorality in the prisons and in the hulks, it is not surprising that the authorities were forced at an early stage to look elsewhere for places to put convicts. In 1846 *The Illustrated London News* described the inside of the hulks:

> The cells throughout the hulk are numbered consecutively, beginning from the lower deck upwards; and prisoners of the worst character, during their period of punishment, are classed in the lower deck, and rise upwards as they progress in character, from the lower to the middle, and from the middle to the upper deck; so that the highest number, containing the men of best character, is on the upper deck.

The Woolwich Warren was a maze of workshops and warehouses where the convicts were put to work. Here the prisoners were employed in shipbuilding and painting, carrying timber for this purpose, removing chain-moorings, cleansing the river banks and in keeping the vessels clean, preparing the food of the convicts generally, and making and repairing their clothes. *HMS Warrior* was a hulk moored at Woolwich. It was built of English oak and served as a seventy-four-gun man of war, taking part in the Battle of Copenhagen. She was also involved in events leading up to the Battle of Trafalgar. In 1818 she became a receiving ship until being purchased by the prison authorities in 1840, after which she was used as a convict ship. The standards of hygiene on board the hulks were so poor that disease spread quickly. Gaol fever (a form of typhus spread by vermin) spread among them and dysentery was also widespread. Hundreds, probably thousands, of convicts died aboard the hulks at Woolwich and their corpses were unceremoniously dumped in the arsenal's marshground. Added to this macabre image was the fact that on warm days the smell of the prisoners, dead and alive, would pollute the river from bank to bank.

In 1851 a mutiny broke out on board the *Warrior*, although this was put down by a detachment of Royal Marines and the prisoners were sent to Millbank Prison.

James Hardy Vaux was a prisoner on the *Retribution* at Woolwich during the early 1800s and gave an account of life on the hulk.

I had now a new scene of misery to contemplate. There were confined in this floating dungeon nearly six hundred men, most of them double-ironed... On arriving on board, we were all immediately stripped, and washed in large tubs of water, then, after putting on each a suit of coarse slop-clothing, we were ironed, and sent below, our own clothes being taken from us... On descending the hatch-way, no conception can be formed of the scene which presented itself.

Every morning, at seven o'clock, all the convicts capable of work... are taken ashore to the Warren, in which the Royal Arsenal and other public buildings are situated, and there employed at various kinds of labour; some of them very fatiguing; and while so employed, each gang of sixteen or twenty men is watched and directed by a fellow called a guard. These guards are commonly of the lowest class of human beings; wretches devoid of feeling; ignorant in the extreme, brutal by nature, and rendered tyrannical and cruel by the consciousness of the power they possess... They invariably carry a large and ponderous stick, with which, without the smallest provocation, they fell an unfortunate convict to the ground, and frequently repeat their blows long after the poor fellow is insensible.

The food the prisoners ate was basic to say the least, and consisted of ox-cheek, either boiled or made into soup, pease and bread or biscuit which were often mouldy. Each prisoner had two pints of beer four days a week and badly filtered water drawn from the river.

Resistance to the closing of the hulks had diminished by 1855 when the Penal Servitude Act ended transportation, replacing it with specific terms of imprisonment in English prisons. On 14 July 1857 *The Times* reported:

At 9 o'clock yesterday morning smoke was observed issuing from the convict hulk *Defense*, moored off Woolwich Arsenal, which, on closer examination was discovered to originate in the fore part of the ship… Every part of the huge vessel was soon filled with smoke and the whole of the inmates were hastily removed.

There had been 171 prisoners aboard up till that day. Many of them were invalids and in the 'last stage of disease'. They were safely evacuated thanks to the prompt action between the warders and the prisoners. All the prisoners were transferred to the convict hulk *Unite* further up the Thames. After eighty years the prison ships had come to an end – or had they? In 1997, the government established a new prison ship, HMP *Weare*, as a temporary measure to ease prison overcrowding. *Weare* was docked at the disused Royal Navy dockyard at Portland, Dorset. On 9 March 2005 it was announced that the *Weare* was to close. Since then, the government has looked into using private contractors to supply prison ship spaces in order to alleviate overcrowding!

Boarding the Convict Ship

After their incarceration on the hulk, the convict's next punishment was to embark upon the ship that would take them on the long journey to Australia.

The journey from hulk or prison to embarkation port was one of public spectacle, as convicts either walked or travelled via carts. Pickpocket George Barrington noted in his journal that he said his farewells and assembled with the others at 4.45 a.m. to be escorted by the city guards from his prison to Blackfriars Bridge. Barrington remarked on the ignominy of being mingled with felons of all descriptions and the humiliation of the early morning walk which would be witnessed by spectators. Even for the renowned thief, this was a 'punishment more severe than the sentence of my country that I had so much wronged'.

Convicts would arrive at Woolwich and Deptford on the Thames dressed in regulation jackets, waistcoats of blue cloth, duck trousers (a durable, closely woven heavy cotton or linen fabric), coarse linen shirts, yarn stockings and woollen caps. Women were issued with a regulation dress, although clothing for the women on the First Fleet in 1787 fell to pieces within weeks of the voyage. In chains, they boarded the ship and were then ordered into the hold where battens were fixed for the hammocks which were hung 'seventeen inches apart'. Barrington, commenting on his feelings, wrote of 'the want of fresh air' which 'rendered [the] situation truly deplorable'.

It was not uncommon for the prisoners to have waited months on the hulks before they embarked onto the convict ship. Psychological and physical trauma was also acknowledged to be a feature of embarkation. Commenting on the adjustment prisoners had to make from Pentonville Prison to convict ship, surgeon John Stephen of the *Sir George Seymour* wrote in 1845:

The sudden change from seclusion to the bustle and noise of a crowded ship produced a number of cases of convulsion, attended in some instances with nausea and vomiting, in others simulating hysteria and in all being of almost anomalous character. The recumbent position, fresh air, mild stimulants etc were found to be beneficial in all cases and after three days the convulsions disappeared.

Conditions in the prison quarters on the ship were cramped, dark, damp and lacking in ventilation. The voyage would present further challenges. In storms and heavy seas the water would sweep through the quarters, which kept the bedding constantly wet. In addition to this were the awful, putrid smells of wet and rotting timbers combined with the packed bodies of the prisoners. In the tropics the heat was unbearable.

Punishments on board varied from whipping, solitary confinement, shaving of heads (a punishment reserved mainly for female convicts), and placing in irons into a small black box for a number of days, to being put on bread and water. In 1832 John Clifton died of exhaustion after being ordered to walk with a bed on his back for two hours – a punishment for expressing his wish that the ship would catch fire. For attempted mutiny, execution was the most serious penalty, although many received a severe flogging. A list of offences that carried punishments was placed on the wall on the prison deck.

Further torments included a range of ailments prisoners would suffer from. Diarrhoea was by far the most common, followed by constipation and haemorrhoids. Large iron buckets were used as toilets, but these could not be emptied and cleaned out during the night. Scurvy, which arises from a lack of vitamin C, became a problem and is mentioned in many of the journals, as did boils, rheumatism, colic and catarrh – convenient catch-all, 'catarrh'. The presence of hordes of rats was an unavoidable hazard; typhus was a dreaded disease facilitated by rats and lice. Cholera was another epidemic disease caused by dirty water.

4

Places Of Execution

Many Londoners were inured to images of death. Public executions, as well as the display of rotting bodies on gibbets and spiked heads on poles, were common sights. Attending an execution was a generally accepted practice, as the diarist Henry Machyn made clear in the mid-sixteenth century: he recorded that he attended two and sometimes three per day. In the space of one month in 1557, Machyn saw eight felons hanged at Tyburn, three men and two women burnt at Smithfield for heresy, and seven pirates hanged at Wapping. Like many Londoners, Machyn witnessed executions as part of the popular calendar ritual.

Smithfield

For over 400 years, Smithfield was one of London's main sites of execution. Smithfield, just to the west of the City of London and close to St Bartholomew's Hospital, is not to be confused with East Smithfield, which was close to the Tower of London and another execution place, albeit minor by comparison. Those whose lives ended at the former included William Wallace, the Scottish patriot, in 1305; many Lollards, religious dissidents of the fourteenth to sixteenth centuries; and numerous Protestant martyrs during the reign of Mary in the middle of the sixteenth century. Those who died for religious reasons were mostly burned as heretics and their sufferings usually attracted large numbers of appalled but fascinated spectators. These times were the heyday of Smithfield as a place of execution, but judicial deaths there continued sporadically into the seventeenth and eighteenth centuries.

The story of William Wallace (1272-1305) has taken on a particular significance in both historical and mythical terms. Conflicts with Scotland from the 1290s saw Wallace establish a reputation. In 1305 Wallace was captured near Glasgow and after a brief imprisonment in Dumbarton Castle he was taken to London to face a show trial in Westminster Hall where he was charged with treason, murder, robbery and 'various other felonies'. The verdict of the court was that Wallace should be dragged from the Palace of Westminster

Gibbet outside Clink Prison.

Smithfield today.

Memorial to William Wallace at Smithfield.

to the Tower of London and from there through the City to Smithfield. On 23 August Wallace was wrapped in an ox hide and dragged by horses four miles through London to Smithfield where he was hanged as a murderer on a very high gallows made for the occasion. An expectant crowd looked on as he was cut down while still alive and then mutilated, disembowelled and, being convicted of treason, his 'privy parts' would have been removed. The ritual continued. As a punishment for the 'great wickedness which he had practised towards God and His holy church by burning churches', his heart, liver, lungs and all internal organs were thrown into the fire and burned. Finally, he was decapitated and his carcass then cut up. His head was set on a pole on London Bridge.

From the fourteenth century a long history of bloody incidents took place at Smithfield. The leader of the Peasants' Revolt of 1382, Wat Tyler, was killed in a confrontation at Smithfield when he was stabbed by the Lord Mayor, William Walworth. Tyler had sought refuge in St Bartholomew's Hospital but was dragged out to be beheaded (it is uncertain whether he was already dead prior to beheading).

The heady days of execution at Smithfield became fewer as Tyburn and later Newgate became the main sites. In 1674, for example, a woman was burned for the crime of clipping (removing precious metal from the edge of coins to melt down).

An unintended 'execution' occurred in 1756. A gang led by James Egan had been responsible for framing and accusing innocent people in order to claim rewards. Their activities had led to prosecutions and the death of some of their victims. Justice eventually caught up with them and Egan and one of the gang, named Salmon, were sentenced to stand in the pillory at Smithfield. This was to be their last public appearance for some time because they had also been condemned to seven years' imprisonment. It was only to be expected that the nature of their crime rendered them exceptionally unpopular with the crowd. Even as they arrived, Egan and Salmon were subjected to a torrent of verbal abuse. No sooner had they been secured in the pillory than they were assailed by a rain of missiles, including stones, cobbles, rotting vegetation and dead, putrescent rats, cats and dogs. The constables tried to intervene but the crowd was growing angrier by the minute. Egan and Salmon were powerless to prevent some of these missiles finding their mark. A large one hit Egan with such force on the forehead that he died instantly.

John Perrot from Newport Pagnell was executed at Smithfield in 1761. He kept a draper's shop and established a reputation as a merchant, and so had little problem in finding credit. Perrott was in fact a wealthy rogue who reputedly embezzled £25,000 of goods received on credit. It was only a matter of time before Perrott's activities would be investigated and he paid a heavy price. At 10.15 a.m. on the morning of 11 November 1761 he said farewell to a fellow prisoner and, with some trembling, was immediately put in the cart and led to Smithfield to be hanged.

Executions at Smithfield ended soon afterwards.

Newgate

Executions began outside Newgate Prison in the street called Old Bailey in 1783. On execution days a scaffold was erected close to the Debtors' Door in the prison wall. Through this door the condemned prisoners were brought for their public swansong. For some this offered a brief moment of celebrity – for once in their lives everybody was interested in them and they were the centre of attention. Later on the scaffold was mounted on wheels and was brought out of Newgate for each execution, drawn by two horses. The first execution in Old Bailey took place on 9 December 1783.

Prisoners varied in the manner in which they approached their execution. Those who excited most admiration from the crowd and even grudgingly from the authorities were those few who refused to be perturbed by the situation and in some cases whistled, sang and joked as if they did not have a care in the world. One murderer named Jeffreys, for example, ordered and was served roast duck the night before his execution and went to his death with a swagger and a cheery wave to the crowd.

Although executions now took place literally on the doorstep of Newgate, a strong sense of carnival surrounded these events. Crowds were as drunken, bawdy and

Punch and Judy can be said to represent the boisterous and anarchic nature of London as well as featuring London hangman Jack Ketch.

irreverent as ever and pickpockets and prostitutes enjoyed rich pickings. Hucksters selling pies, fried fish and all manner of snacks and beverages elbowed their way through the teeming crowds, doing a roaring trade.

On the night before an execution, the peace of the small hours would be disturbed by the sounds of revelry from those who had arrived early to get the best view of the morning's proceedings. The noise they made would have been audible to the occupants of the condemned cells eking out their last hours. From the condemned cells the prisoners were taken to the Long Room where they were met by a crowd of officials, newspaper reporters and others who had managed to insinuate themselves into the occasion. The irons were struck off the prisoners and their arms were tightly bound. The chaplain or ordinary would be annoying everyone by trying to get the prisoner to blurt out a confession, but all that most prisoners were capable of at this stage was sobbing, sighing or sometimes a frenzied last-minute appeal for clemency. A procession then formed up composed of sheriffs, warders, the hangman and assistants, guards and the prisoner or prisoners and they emerged into Old Bailey through the Debtors' Door. They were met with a great roar from the crowd, temporarily drowning out the solemn toll of the bell of St Sepulchre's Church nearby. A cry of 'Hats off, Hats off' reverberated through the crowd as headwear was doffed and everyone jostled in the confined space in order to get the best view possible.

The keenest enthusiasts for a hanging often arrived in Old Bailey the evening before so as to obtain ringside seats. Sometimes there were enough of them to create an unruly mob which spent the night singing, dancing, drinking and, if the mood developed, in brazenly overt individual and group sex sessions. The Governor of Newgate invited friends and family to an exclusive social event in a room with an excellent view overlooking Old Bailey. The ritual was to have a few drinks and then watch and hopefully enjoy the hanging. This was followed by a hearty breakfast which traditionally always included grilled or devilled kidneys. Having gorged themselves, the party then watched the cutting down of the corpse (which took place an hour after the felon's death). Rooms with a view of proceedings could also be hired, at very considerable expense, in the Magpie and Stump pub in Old Bailey. They advertised 'execution breakfasts'.

In 1820 the Cato Street Conspirators, who had plotted to assassinate the entire Cabinet, were the last people to be publicly decapitated. A large crowd gathered outside Newgate. When the executioner raised one of the severed heads to show the crowd and then managed to drop it, there was a chorus of derisory catcalls and shouts of 'Butterfingers'.

The last execution outside Newgate took place on 26 May 1868 when hangman Calcraft terminated the life of a young Irish republican called Michael Barrett who had tried to blow up the Middlesex House of Detention in Clerkenwell in order to rescue some fellow nationalists who were detained there. A spectacular explosion brought down some of the prison walls but also demolished a terrace of houses opposite, killing six people immediately and fatally injuring others. For all this effort, the Irish nationalists remained immured in their cells. This was the last public execution in Britain. Hangings within Newgate ended in 1902.

Tyburn

Tyburn was London's major place of execution for hundreds of years. Although it is now very close to the permanent traffic pandemonium around Marble Arch, when Tyburn was used for executions it was a rural spot along the muddy lane which was the old Roman road leading to Oxford. It was about three miles west of the City of London.

It is thought that the first executions took place at Tyburn around 1196, and from that time many thousands of condemned prisoners ended their days at this spot. They were from all classes and had been found guilty of every kind of capital offence. In 1571 the legendary 'Triple Tree' was erected at Tyburn. This was a triangular gallows capable of hanging twenty-four people at a time, eight on each beam. It operated until 1759, when it was replaced by a movable scaffold.

One of the most extraordinary sights at Tyburn was the public hanging of the dead bodies of three of the 'regicides' who were held responsible for signing the death warrant of Charles I. On 30 January 1662 the corpses of Oliver Cromwell, Henry Ireton (his son-in-law) and John Bradshaw, the judge at Charles's trial, were hanged publicly on the 'Triple Tree' then cut down, decapitated and thrown into a nearby pit.

Persons convicted of larceny, burglary, housebreaking, pick-pocketing and highway robbery feature largely on the list of the tens of thousands who died at Tyburn while murderers, arsonists, rapists, bigamists and those found guilty of treason were also executed there, but in smaller numbers. In the fifteenth and seventeenth centuries many were executed for their religion, having been found guilty of either heresy or treason. Witchcraft and infanticide became capital offences in the sixteenth and seventeenth centuries and so the perpetrators of such offences made their unhappy way to Tyburn.

Hangings at Tyburn usually took place on the first Monday of each month. On every execution day, thousands would line the route or make their way to Tyburn to watch and enjoy the proceedings. If the felon(s) to be hanged were particularly notorious, hated or popular with the citizenry then tens or even hundreds of thousands would turn out and the route from Newgate to Tyburn and the surroundings of the gallows would be *en fête*. Those who might have described themselves as aficionados of hangings would set great store by the conduct and bearing of those who were about to be hanged. Prisoners were allowed to make

Hogarth's illustration of Tyburn and its crowd.

Marble Arch, near to the old Tyburn gallows.

a last-minute speech from the gallows. Those so terrified they were scarcely able to stand but who mumbled out a cringing confession or a hopeless appeal for clemency did so to a chorus of catcalls and ribaldry. Those felons who used the occasion to boast of their crimes or to attack the authorities for their corruption were always guaranteed a warm reception. The hangman and his assistants were almost universally jeered at and booed unless the felon they were about to hang had been found guilty of an unacceptable crime such as child molestation, in which case they became heroes for the day. Such was the demand for a good view of the proceedings at Tyburn that a permanent grandstand was erected, the enterprising owners of which were able to charge fees for entry dependent on the notoriety or otherwise of the felon(s) being hanged on the day.

The last execution at Tyburn was on 29 August 1783, after which such events were transferred to the outside of Newgate Prison. This change had nothing to do with more humane or enlightened attitudes to penal policy, but was because the execution days had become associated with disorder which upset trade and commerce in the City and along the route to Tyburn. Additionally, the residents of the highly fashionable streets and squares being developed north and south of what is now Oxford Street objected to the presence of the unruly and irreverent crowds that gathered every hanging day. The decision to end the spectacle of the procession

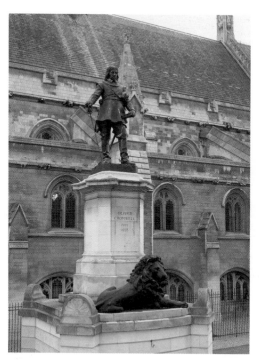

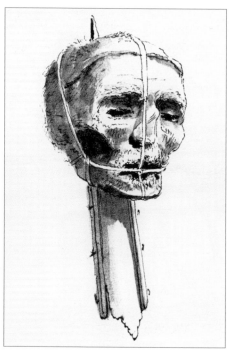

Statue of Oliver Cromwell outside the Houses of Parliament.

A drawing of Cromwell's head, now interred in the wall of Sidney Sussex College Chapel at Cambridge.

from Newgate and the executions at Tyburn did not, however, meet with universal approval: Dr Johnson in particular fulminated that 'the old method drew together a number of spectators. The old method was most satisfactory for all parties: the public was gratified by the procession; the criminal was supported by it. Why has all this to be swept away?'

The procession through the streets from Newgate to Tyburn and the events there had many of the elements of a carnival. The 'Hanging Days' gave people a break from everyday drudgery and it gave them an opportunity to mock their so-called social superiors. The whole ritual, including the selling of food, drink and broadsheets with the supposed 'last confessions' of the condemned prisoner, the opportunities for pickpockets, the drunken revelry and the fights, the last speech from the scaffold, the undignified scramble that sometimes took place to prevent the surgeons getting hold of the body – all these were part of a performance. The image is vividly portrayed by William Hogarth in his *The Idle 'Prentice executed at Tyburn* which depicts a scene which has little to do with submission to, or respect for, the power of the State as demonstrated by a judicial hanging.

As Francis Place, the political radical, remarked, 'a hanging day was to all intents and purposes a fair day'.

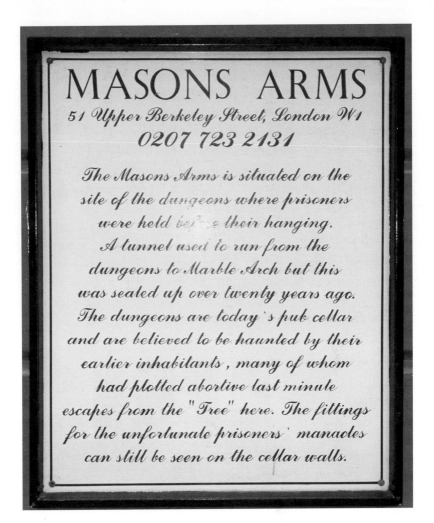

MASONS ARMS

51 Upper Berkeley Street, London W1

0207 723 2131

The Masons Arms is situated on the site of the dungeons where prisoners were held before their hanging. A tunnel used to run from the dungeons to Marble Arch but this was sealed up over twenty years ago. The dungeons are today's pub cellar and are believed to be haunted by their earlier inhabitants, many of whom had plotted abortive last minute escapes from the "Tree" here. The fittings for the unfortunate prisoners' manacles can still be seen on the cellar walls.

Sign outside the Masons Arms near Marble Arch.

Black humour was an essential feature of public executions and various slang terms emerged to describe various aspects of the event. It was a 'hanging match', a 'collar day' or the 'Paddington Fair'. To be hanged was 'to dance the Paddington frisk', to be 'collared', 'nubbed, 'stretched', 'tucked up' or 'turned off'. Also common were such sayings as, 'a man hanged will piss when he cannot whistle' and 'there is nothing to being hang'd but a wry neck and a wet pair of breeches'.

For officialdom the main purpose of the public hanging was to demonstrate the awful consequences that followed conviction for serious offences. Executions supposedly showed the power of the State and acted as a deterrent to crime for those who attended them.

In the eighteenth century, however, an increasing number of dissident voices were heard, questioning the deterrent effect, especially given the number of pickpockets plying their criminal trade among the crowds who were perhaps watching the dying moments of a felon condemned to death for the self-same offence. Henry Grattan (1746-1820), a reforming MP, said, 'The more you hang, the more you transport, the more you inflame, disturb and disaffect'. After the simultaneous execution of eleven felons at Tyburn was followed by a spate of street robberies the following night, Henry Fielding, the novelist and reforming magistrate, observed, '...the execution of criminals as presently conducted, serve, I apprehend, a purpose diametrically opposed to that for which they were designed; and tend to inspire the vulgar with a contempt of the gallows rather than a fear of it'. Others asked whether repeated viewings of institutionalised State violence did not simply make those who observed them indifferent to the spectacle. The fact is that Londoners were inured to images of death. In 1847 a journalist wrote, 'We have seen every execution for the past ten years and boast how on one day we saw one man hung at Newgate and took a cab to Horsemonger Lane in time to see another'. Dickens, watching the execution of a murderer, commented sorrowfully that the crowd displayed 'no sorrow, no salutary terror, no observance, no seriousness; nothing but ribaldry, debauchery, levity, drunkenness, and flaunting vice in fifty other shapes'.

The Carpenters Arms near Marble Arch, which was said to have bought the old movable gallows and used for them as stands for beer barrels.

It is not surprising that the authorities eventually withdrew hangings from the public gaze. The scaffold crowds had adamantly refused to play the role expected of them. They appropriated the occasion for their own purposes. They protested, they scoffed, they mocked, they were irreverent and at times their behaviour became riotous enough to alarm the forces of law and order. The State might have controlled the theatre of punishment, but it had little hold over what happened during the performance. On one occasion, when two political radicals popular with the spectators were hanged, the *Gentlemen's Magazine* indignantly reported that 'the mob on this occasion behaved outrageously, insulted the Sheriffs, pulled up the gallows, broke the windows, destroyed the furniture, and committed other outrages'.

Charing Cross

A number of significant executions took place at Charing Cross during the seventeenth century. In 1544 William John Tooley, a poulterer, robbed a Spaniard in St James. Tooley was taken to Charing Cross in a cart before a large crowd to be hanged. However, the most gruesome executions were those of the regicides in 1660.

Of the fifty-nine men who signed Charles I's death warrant, forty-one were still alive and of these, fifteen fled the country. Ten were condemned to death at Charing Cross and Tyburn, in October 1660. On Saturday 13 October 1660, between nine and ten o'clock in the morning, Major-General Thomas Harrison was drawn upon a hurdle from Newgate to Charing Cross where a scaffold had been erected. He was the first of the regicides to face the brutal punishment. He was hanged with his face looking towards the Banqueting-house at Whitehall. Being half dead, he was cut down by the executioner, and then 'his Privy Members cut off before his eyes, his Bowels burned, his Head severed from his Body, and his Body divided into Quarters, which were returned back to Newgate upon the same Hurdle that carried it'. In traditional manner his head was set upon a pole on the top of the south-east end of Westminster Hall and his quarters were hanged upon the city gates.

On 16 October John Cooke, the chief prosecutor at the trial, and Hugh Peters were also executed at Charing Cross. After the former's last words he was quickly taken from the rope and stripped of his clothes. His genitals were removed and held before his eyes and then the lining of his inner bowel was twisted out. Cooke looked on as his entrails were burned. Hugh Peters (1598–1660) was observed to be drinking some cordial liquors to keep him from fainting. Peters had to sit and watch Cooke go through the agonies of execution. The executioner, covered in blood, approached Peters 'and rubbing his bloody hands together asked, "how do you like this Mr Peters, how do you like my work?"' The stench that emanated from the burning of the intestines brought complaints from the residents and the executions of the regicides Axtell and Hacker were moved to Tyburn.

The barbaric death by hanging, drawing and quartering.

Other Places of Public Execution

Many other locations in London saw public executions. A few are mentioned below.

Charles I was executed at Whitehall on 30 January 1649. The shock waves from the unprecedented judicial execution of one of God's anointed reverberated around Western Europe and threatened wars of intervention.

On Tuesday 30 January 1649, a bitterly cold day, Charles went to his death. He entered the Banqueting House, walked through the Banqueting Hall and proceeded to the scaffold which had been erected outside one of the windows of the palace. The scaffold was draped in black and the floor likewise, and the axe and the block laid in the middle of the scaffold. The block was about 1ft high. Charles delivered his last speech, then spoke to the executioner and said, 'I shall say but very short prayers and then thrust out my hands', indicating this was the sign to bring down the axe. He then stooped down, laid his neck upon the block and after a short pause stretched out his hands. The executioner with one blow severed Charles' head from his body and then held it up to the crowd and shouted 'Behold the head of a traitor!' An eye-witness recorded that as the King's head fell, 'There was such a groan by the thousands then present as I have never heard before and desire I may never hear again'.

Several of those implicated in the Gunpowder Plot of 1605 were executed in the old Palace-Yard at Westminster. Sir Walter Raleigh was executed in the same place in 1618.

The Tower of London is almost synonymous with the spectre of human misery, imprisonment, mutilation, torture and execution. Those who were executed on

HIS MAJESTY KING CHARLES I
PASSED THROUGH THIS HALL AND
OUT OF A WINDOW NEARLY OVER
THIS TABLET TO THE SCAFFOLD
IN WHITEHALL WHERE HE WAS
BEHEADED ON 30ᵗʰ JANUARY 1649

Bust of King Charles I outside the
Banqueting House, Whitehall.

Tower Green were usually political prisoners whose arraignment was controversial or delicate enough to make it expedient for them to be disposed of within the high security offered by the Tower's precincts. Among those who breathed their last on Tower Green courtesy of the executioner was Anne Boleyn, decapitated with a sword in 1536, it being said that a man capable of doing the task had to be sent for from Calais. Another of Henry's wives, Catherine Howard, followed in 1542, and Lady Jane Grey in 1554. Robert Devereux, one-time favourite of Elizabeth I, was despatched in 1601.

Tower Hill was a slightly elevated site close to the Tower. About 125 people are thought to have been executed there, the majority for treasonable activity or because the authorities thought their existence constituted a political threat. In 1381, during the Peasants' Revolt, the hated Archbishop of Canterbury, Simon of Sudbury, was put to death at Tower Hill by the insurgents. Thomas More, previously one of Henry VIII's closest advisors, was executed by order of the King on 6 July 1535. There were considerable risks attached to being one of Henry's advisors – as Thomas Cromwell found to his cost in July 1540. In 1631 the Earl of Castlehaven was beheaded at Tower Hill. He had assisted the raping of his own wife by two of his servants, forced his wife to have sex with other servants while he watched and forced his daughter, aged twelve, to have sex with the servants. He in turn buggered some of the servants. An especially large crowd turned out to watch him being despatched. The hated favourite of Charles I, Thomas Wentworth, Earl of Strafford, was executed to popular acclaim in 1641.

Execution at Execution Dock, Wapping.

A mixture of references including the Tyburn gallows, Kennington Common gibbet and the bell that tolled for the condemned at St Sepulchre's, Newgate.

An execution on the roof of Horsemonger Lane Gaol.

The dock in Wapping had a special role to play in the history of London executions. This was where pirates and others who had committed capital offences on tidal waters or waters under the jurisdiction of the Admiralty paid for their crimes. This spot, about a mile east of the Tower, became known as 'Execution Dock'. Perhaps its best-known victim was Captain Kidd, a man for whom the words bloodcurdling and swashbuckling might have been invented, but whose career was actually rather more like that of the cartoon character Captain Pugwash. He was hanged in 1701. The last hanging here occurred in 1831. A curious practice was that the hanging took place at the low-water mark and the corpse of the victim was left in place until three high tides had washed over them. This probably meant that during the period in which the corpse was visible, it would have been seen by large numbers of mariners for whom the consequences of piracy would be abundantly obvious.

Among other places north of the Thames where executions were carried out were: Old Mitre Court, off Fleet Street; the junction of Haymarket and Panton Street in what is now SW1; Leadenhall Street, Cheapside; St Paul's Churchyard, St Giles-in-the-Fields; and Clerkenwell Green. On occasions, condemned felons were executed at the scene of their crimes and so there are many other one-off locations where such events have taken place.

South of the Thames, a number of executions were carried out at Kennington Common.

Horsemonger Lane was the name commonly used for the Surrey County Gaol built in Southwark in the 1770s. A particularly famous execution was that of the husband and wife, Mr and Mrs Manning (the first in England since 1700 of a married couple) who were hanged in 1849 for murdering Patrick O'Connor. The couple had incurred financial loss as a result of bad financial advice given by O'Connor. The latter was attacked with a chisel and then finished off with a bullet, after which he was buried under the kitchen floor. The hanging of the Mannings was watched

The site of Horsemonger Lane Gaol.

by Charles Dickens, who was disgusted by the animalistic behaviour of the crowd baying for the blood of this singularly repulsive pair of murderers. Dickens did not know which was worse, the appearance of the Mannings in their death-throes or the expectant faces in the crowd.

On 16 April 1862 James Longhurst was hanged at Horsemonger Lane for murdering a girl of seven. The heinousness of his crime ensured an especially large and hostile crowd.

Horsemonger Lane Gaol closed in 1878 and Newington Recreation Ground now covers the site.

5

Methods and Instruments of Torture and Execution

It is a serious mistake to consider instruments of torture as quaint relics of the past which can be viewed with amused detachment by those who visit castle dungeons or museums of crime and punishment. Torture, or the threat of it, has long been used as a means of breaking resistance and extracting information; doubtless it will continue to be used until such time as man moves onto a better and higher form of society.

It is sometimes difficult to distinguish between an instrument of punishment and of torture or execution, so we will be fairly ecumenical and not too prescriptive in what we present below. It is likely that all the methods and instruments mentioned below have been employed in London in the past but that is not to say that they are unique to the metropolis. It is also likely that all of them, in similar or adapted form, have extracted their toll of human misery somewhere else in these islands.

Hanging

The earliest judicial hangings simply used the branch of a convenient tree. More permanent arrangements involved uprights and a crossbeam. The victims climbed a ladder and had a rope placed around their necks. When all was ready, the ladders were turned round and removed; hence the victims being 'turned off'. In the endless drive for greater efficiency, later on the victims were placed standing on a cart, likewise with a rope around their necks hanging from a crossbeam. The horse would then be whipped and as the cart shuttled away, the prisoners were left dangling in mid-air. In 1760 the device known as 'the drop' was introduced, first used at the Tower. Now the victim stood on a trap door on the scaffold. When the bolt was drawn, the trap door opened and the victim fell through to eternity. Some teething problems were encountered but when these were overcome, it was widely believed that the drop brought death to the victim more quickly.

The London Dungeon on Tooley Street, London Bridge, dedicated to the display of punishments from London's history.

Hanging days were occasions for joyful revelry – at least for those who turned out to watch proceedings if not, of course, for the condemned prisoners, their friends and relations. Death by strangulation was slow – anything up to twenty minutes in some cases although unconsciousness came somewhat sooner. The crowds seem to have enjoyed watching the felon choking out the last few minutes of his life but sometimes they were thwarted in their voyeurism when, for an agreed sum, the hangman allowed the victim's relations to pull on his legs, thereby shortening his suffering. To present-day tastes, the whole public performance and the rituals that went with it seem barbaric, especially since the victims often involuntarily evacuated their bladders and bowels.

Beheading

Beheading has been carried out with a sword or an axe. Very considerable skill is required by the executioner if beheading is to be done in such a way as to minimise the suffering of the victim. Long and assiduous practice on dummies or animals in slaughterhouses was needed by the axeman because the neck presents only a small target for a rapidly descending axe brought down from over the back of the head. Likewise, decapitation with the sword can only be done effectively after a prolonged apprenticeship. It is in recognition of the fact that an expert wielding the sword or the axe can bring about an almost instantaneous death that these methods have been regarded as the prerogative of the high-born. The lower echelons of society have had to put up with the altogether slower and frequently more uncertain ministrations of the hangman.

There was nothing very subtle about the headsman's axe. Its action was basically like that of a chisel, crushing its way through the vertebrae by brute force as the heavy instrument descended on the neck. Its blunt edge is not intended for cutting but for breaking. It was

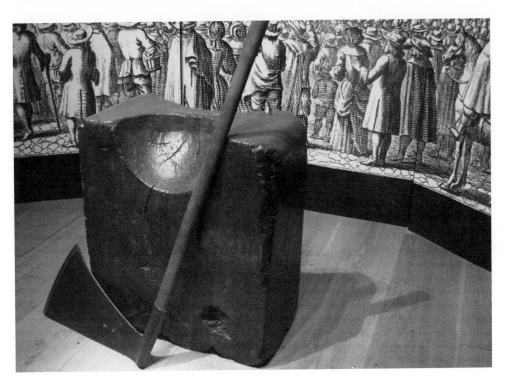

Block and axe in the Tower of London.

all very well for the headsman to while away his spare time practising, but unfortunately even the most extrovert of operatives sometimes withered under the critical eye of the kind of people who turned up at executions. Some of the spectators were hardened veterans of hundreds of executions and they put the headsman's performance under almost as much critical scrutiny as they bestowed on the behaviour and demeanour of the person being executed. Under these circumstances, headsmen sometimes became nervous and they might bungle the beheading, needing several blows with the axe to complete the operation. If this happened, it would be to an accompaniment of derisory scoffing from the audience and heart-rending screams of agony from the not-quite deceased. It was clearly in the latter's interest to have the job completed as quickly and simply as possible and victims frequently offered the headsman money as an incentive to ensure a job well done.

When the head was severed, it was normal for the executioner to hold it up for the crowd to see that the deed had been properly completed. Later, the head was sewn back on for the sake of appearances. The executioner would accompany the act by a statement such as, 'Behold the head of a traitor!' At least one severed head is supposed to have snarled back a statement such as, 'You lie, I am no traitor!' This ritual was important because it provided evidence of death and supposedly prevented an impostor coming forward at a later stage.

THE TRUE MANER OF THE EXECUTION OF THOMAS EARLE OF STRAFFORD. LORD
Lieutenant of Ireland. vpon Tower hill. the 12ᵗ of May. 1641.
HYBERNIÆ PROREGIS SVPPLICIVM·

A. Doctor Vſher, Lord Prima.
te of Ireland.
B the Sherifes of London
C the Earle of Strafford.
D. his Kindred and Friends.

Execution des Grafen Thomæ von Stafford Statthalters in Irland auf dẽ Tawers plah in Londen 12 Maj 1641.
A. Doct. Uſher Primat in Irland.   C. Der Graf von Stafford.
B. Rahts Herren von Londen.   D. Seine anverwänten ynd freünde.

The execution of the Earl of Strafford in 1641; a crowd of over 100,000 was reputed to have attended.

The block was of course the axe's partner in crime and it evolved over the years from a plain log into something specially shaped for its purpose. It was usually about 2ft high and designed so that the head fell off into a waiting basket of sawdust. If the first blow inflicted a deep but not fatal wound, severing the artery, it was by no means unknown for those close by to be sprayed by high-pressure blood.

Death by Burning

This was the punishment largely reserved for heretics. The theory was that they had been guilty of thought-crime, of holding and practising unacceptable religious ideas, and that death by burning was a condign preparation for the fires waiting for them in Hell. The burning was a symbolic destruction of the evil ideas the person harboured as well as the death of the reprobate himself.

Witches and women found guilty of murdering their husbands were also burned to death. It seems almost inconceivable by modern standards, but burning was devised as a method of execution for women to protect their modesty! It was though that public hanging, drawing and quartering would be indelicate as parts of their bodies would be exposed to public gaze.

Death by burning.

The victim was tied to a stake with a rope around her neck and at the agreed moment the executioner ignited the firewood and tugged on the rope. The theory was that the victim would be dead by the time the flames were licking around her body. However, in the case of Catherine Hayes, who was executed at Tyburn in 1726 for killing her husband, the wood flared up so quickly that the executioner had to remove himself before strangulation was complete. The crowd was then treated to the sight of Catherine's prolonged and excruciating death agonies. The executioner had little option but to pile on more faggots hoping that the conflagration would be intense enough to shorten her sufferings.

Death by Boiling

Perhaps fortunately, the authorities did not often have recourse to this diabolical form of execution. Seemingly the first person to suffer this fate was one Richard Rose in 1531. He was a cook who was found guilty of high treason for poisoning the family and household of the Bishop of Rochester. Seventeen people suffered severely and two actually died. Rose was placed in an iron cauldron of water over a fire which was then brought to the boil. He took two hours to die in full public view at Smithfield. It was assumed that the poisoning was deliberate. Modern scientific techniques might instead have detected poor hygiene standards or even a dose of salmonella.

The horror of death by this singularly unpleasant, but fortunately rare, method was perhaps slightly lessened in later years when the victim was placed in water that was already at boiling point. Would that actually be any better?

Gibbeting

The English were not known to be particularly fastidious when it came to the methods of punishment and execution they employed. However, it does seem that unlike their counterparts in some European countries, they did not very often gibbet people alive. Instead, they usually employed gibbeting as a kind of aggravated punishment with the added bonus that it was believed to be a deterrent to wrongdoing on the part of those whose glance fell on the gruesome remains of some miscreant swaying to and fro in an iron cage caught up by the wind. Certain types of offender – highwaymen and pirates in particular – had their bodies daubed in tar or some other preservative substance after death, whereupon they were placed in chains inside a hanging iron cage and displayed in some conspicuous place such as a crossroads or, in the case of the pirates, a prominent spot near a river frequented by large numbers of passing ships.

The fleshy parts of the gibbeted cadaver and such items as the eyes soon disappeared thanks to the attentions of birds, especially of the crow family, and rats, which were not averse to making their way up the wooden supports into the cage where the corpse provided, literally, easy meat. Such corpses soon became little more than a collection of bones, which often collapsed and often fell out of the cage to gladden the hearts of passing dogs.

The Judas Cradle

Just because no one in English officialdom has ever admitted that this diabolical procedure has been used, we cannot therefore assume that it has not. England had all manner of close links with governments in Western Europe in medieval times and word got about. The Judas Cradle was such a simple, economical and effective means for extracting information that it somewhat stretches the bounds of credibility to think that this device never lurked in the darkest and dingiest dungeon of the Tower of London.

The victim had his hands tied behind his back and was secured in an iron waist ring. He was then hoisted up by a system of winches and pulleys only to be lowered onto the sharp point of a pyramid surmounting a sturdy tripod. The victim was placed in such a way that his or her weight rested on the apex of the pyramid positioned in the anus, in the vagina, under the scrotum or the coccyx. The torturer responded to the requirements of the interrogator by varying the pressure being applied and could rock the victim or make him fall repeatedly on the point.

The Cat O' Nine Tails

This instrument was used as a means of punishment in the Royal Navy, whose ships were frequently to be seen around Deptford Dockyard and occasionally in the Pool of London. A somewhat lighter version was used in the Army. The naval cat had a handle of rope or sometimes of wood about 2ft long and 1in in diameter. Each of the nine tails or thongs was ¼in in diameter and 2ft long. They usually had one or two knots along their length.

The crew would be assembled to witness the punishment, with marines standing by with muskets and fixed bayonets. The offender was tied to an upright grating and stripped to the waist. Punishment was then inflicted by the bosun's mates and the lashes were usually administered in multiples of six. The knots in the tails had the effect of lacerating the skin in a prolonged flogging and on occasions the flesh was stripped away to reveal the bones. When punishment was completed, the offender was cut down and usually swabbed with salt water to stem the bleeding.

The cat was sometimes used in civil prisons.

The Scavenger's Daughter

On display in the White Tower at the Tower of London is this device also known as 'Skeffington's Gyves'. Leonard Skeffington was a Lieutenant of the Tower in the 1530s (though he is more likely to have adapted an existing device than to have invented one himself). Made of iron, this fiendish apparatus had spaces for the neck, the wrists and the ankles and it had the effect of compressing the body of the victim, inducing excruciating pain, especially in the abdominal and rectal areas. Its advocates considered that it induced more pain than the rack. It was probably the ideal torture machine. It was light and easily transported, and the mere sight of it was often enough to persuade a prisoner to cooperate fully with his inquisitors.

Whipping

Whipping was an economical punishment since little capital outlay was required. A common practice was 'whipping at the cart's tail'. The offender was stripped to the waist and tied to the back of a horse-drawn wagon. As the horse drew the wagon and the offender slowly through the streets, whipping would be administered at prescribed places, particularly at the scene of the crime. The more serious the offence, the longer the journey around town. This punishment involved public humiliation as well as pain. Sometimes the public were allowed to whip the offender as he passed by where they were standing. Whippings or floggings with a birch were also administered for various misdemeanours in prison.

Mutilation

Tongues that had uttered blasphemous, treasonable or otherwise unacceptable words might be ripped out or have a hole bored in them. The hand of a thief or assailant might be removed. The punishment of time in the pillory might be aggravated by the offender having his ears nailed to the woodwork. Prostitutes sometimes had their noses slit – perhaps this was intended to be bad for their business activities.

Branding

Branding was a handy punishment, combining as it did the administering of pain with the depositing of a permanent visible scar or stigma. Different letters were burned into the flesh to signify different offences. A 'V' indicated a runaway servant while 'T' was a thief and 'FA' was a false accuser. The law banned civil branding in 1829. Vagrants were frequently branded, which often made it difficult for them to ever become gainfully employed.

The Rack

The rack was used in the Tower of London to extort information and 'confessions' from, among others, those who thought up the Gunpowder Plot in 1605. The victim was tightly secured to a table and attached to an apparatus which literally stretched him – several inches. The pull exerted was usually comparatively gentle at first but would be intensified by the torturer if he felt that his victim was holding back vital information. Every joint in the arms and legs would be dislocated, the spinal column dismembered and the muscles of the limbs, thorax and abdomen ripped apart. This appalling device served the purposes of the interrogator, the torturer and the executioner.

6

The Pillory

The pillory was another form of torture, although on rare occasions those subjected to such punishment were 'rewarded' by the crowd who laid flowers at their feet or even collected money for them. Stocks and pillories were used in parts of Europe for more than 1,000 years. They became common in England by the mid-fourteenth century. In 1351 a law (Statute of Labourers) was introduced requiring every town to provide and maintain a set of stocks. The pillory was a device made of a wooden or metal framework erected on a post, with holes for securing the head and hands in which the convicted person would face the wrath of the public.

A stock is simply a wooden board with one or more semicircles cut into one edge. Initially used for quacks and mountebanks, stocks were later used to control the unemployed. In 1287 Robert Basset, Mayor of London, punished bakers for making underweight bread. A number of them were put in the pillory, as was Agnes Daintie, for selling 'mingled butter'. A statute passed in 1495 required that vagabonds should be set in the stocks for three days on bread and water and then sent away. A further statute of 1605 required that anyone convicted of drunkenness should receive six hours in the stocks. After 1637, it became the recognised punishment for those who published books without a licence or criticised the government. The pillory was abolished in England in 1837.

The status of the pillory was elevated from a punishment reserved for cheats, thieves and perjurers to one which also punished those involved in political disputes. This was due to the work of the Archbishop of Canterbury William Laud (1573-1645) and the Star Chamber in 1637.

In the same year a high profile case saw the brutal punishment of three Puritan preachers: William Prynne, Henry Burton and John Bastwick. In the growing discontent prior to the Civil Wars they were prosecuted by Star Chamber for publishing pamphlets attacking the rule of the bishops and criticising the doctrines of Archbishop Laud. All three were sentenced to stand in Palace Yard in the pillory and have their cheeks branded and ears cropped before being imprisoned for life. The following account gives a graphic description of what happened:

William Prynne, who had his ears lopped off in 1637.

Dr Bastwick spake first, and (among other things) said, had he a thousand lives he would give them all up for this cause. Mr Prynne... showed the disparity between the times of Queen Mary and Queen Elizabeth, and the times then [of King Charles], and how far more dangerous it was now to write against a bishop or two than against a King or Queen: there at the most there was but six months imprisonment in ordinary prisons, and the delinquent might redeem his ears for £200, and had two months' time for payment, but no fine; here they are fined £5,000 a piece, to be perpetually imprisoned in the remotest castles, where no friends must be permitted to see them, and to lose their ears without redemption. There no stigmatizing, here he must be branded on both cheeks... The Archbishop of Canterbury, being informed by his spies what Mr Prynne said, moved the Lords then sitting in the Star Chamber that he might be gagged and have some further censure to be presently executed on him; but that motion did not succeed. Mr Burton spake much while in the pillory to the people. The executioner cut off his ears deep and close, in a cruel manner, with much effusion of blood, an artery being cut, as there was likewise of Dr Bastwick. Then Mr Prynne's cheeks were seared with an iron made exceeding hot which done, the executioner cut off one of his ears and a piece of his cheek with it; then hacking the other ear almost off, he left it hanging and went down; but being called up again he cut it quite off. [Source: John Rushworth (1706, abridged edition) *Historical Collections*, volume two, pp. 293]

The following year, political radical and Leveller John Lilburne (1614-1657) was charged with printing and circulating unlicensed books. He was found guilty and

Henry Burton, who was publicly mutilated in 1637.

fined £500, whipped, pilloried and imprisoned. He was whipped from Fleet Prison to Palace Yard. When he was placed in the pillory he tried to make a speech and distribute pamphlets…

The Quaker James Nayler rode into Bristol on a donkey in 1656, imitating Christ's entry into Jerusalem. For this act the government, in December 1656, declared him guilty of blasphemy. Some MPs demanded that he should be stoned to death in accordance with the Old Testament penalty for blasphemy. Nayler was taken to the pillory at Westminster and then whipped through the streets to the Old Exchange, where he stood again in the pillory for two hours. He then had his tongue bored through with a red-hot iron and was branded on the forehead with the letter 'B' for blasphemer. He was then returned to Bristol and made to repeat his ride while facing the rear of his horse. Finally, he was taken back to London and committed to solitary confinement in Bridewell for an indefinite period.

Titus Oates (1649-1705) was an Anglican priest who claimed there was a Jesuit-led plan to assassinate Charles II in order to hasten the succession of the Catholic James. Oates' story was a complete fabrication, but it was sufficient to create a scare as well as sending a number of innocent men to their deaths at Tyburn. These events sparked a wave of anti-Catholic persecution with thirty-five innocent people executed and hundreds of others suffering as a consequence of Oates' claims. In sentencing Oates, Judge Withers said, 'I never pronounce criminal sentence but with some compassion; but you are such a villain and hardened sinner, that I can find no sentiment of compassion for you'. Found guilty of perjury on two separate indictments, he was

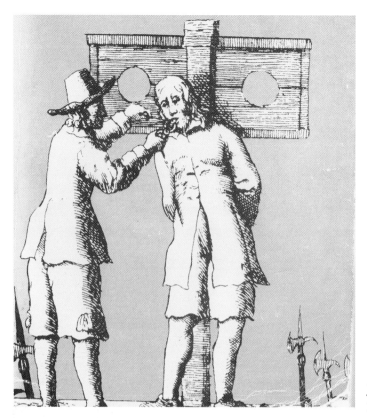

James Nayler being
punished in the pillory.

condemned in 1685 to public exposure on three consecutive days. According to his
sentence, Oates was to stand every year of his life in the pillory on five different days:
before the gate of Westminster Hall, at Charing Cross, at the Temple, at the Royal
Exchange and at Tyburn. However, the government eventually made the infamous
villain a pensioner.

The crowd did not always respond in a brutal way. The *Post Boy* newspaper recorded
that Tristrum Savage stood in the pillory in June 1702 at the 'Chancery Lane end in
Fleet Street, for publishing a scandalous paper, called, The Black List, and some people
had the confidence to give him wine and money as he stood in the pillory'.

Likewise with Daniel Defoe, famous for his novel *Robinson Crusoe* (1719): in 1703,
the government offered a reward of fifty pounds for the arrest of Defoe for being the
author of a 'scandalous and seditious' pamphlet which lampooned the Church. Defoe
gave himself up and was sentenced to be pilloried three times. On 29 July he stood in
the pillory at Cheapside, two days later in the Temple, Fleet Street. Here he met with
a sympathetic crowd who flung garlands, instead of rotten eggs and garbage at the
pamphleteer and drank his health.

In June 1732 the robber John Waller was sentenced to stand twice in the pillory
at Seven Dials, bareheaded, with his crime written in large characters. He did not

reach his second stint in the pillory. Such was the indignation of the populace that they pelted him to death. The day after, the coroner's inquest gave a verdict of 'Willful murder by persons unknown'.

The attitude towards homosexuals was vicious, as newspaper accounts confirm. In January 1727 Robert Whale and York Horner were found guilty of sodomy and for keeping a 'House for the Entertainment of Sodomites'. Their punishment was to stand in the famous pillory at Charing Cross. One month later the London Journal (7 February) reported that Peter Dubourg stood in the 'Pillory at the Royal-Exchange, for attempting to commit Sodomy; and was severely treated by the populace'. In April 1727 Charles Hitchin, City Marshal, was committed to Newgate by Justice Haynes for the 'odious and detestable Sin of Sodomy, committed on the Body of Richard

The hated Titus Oates
stands in the pillory.

Williamson' (*Daily Post*). He was sentenced to stand in the pillory in the Strand. His punishment took place in May but his friends attempted to intervene. They barricaded the avenues leading to him with coaches and carts, rendering any 'approaches by the Mob inaccessible' (*The Weekly Journal: or, The British Gazetteer,* 6 May). However, the attempt to repel 'the Fury of the Populace proved ineffectual. He was taken down at the usual Time, and carried back to Newgate, almost ready to expire, with the Fatigue he had undergone in the Rostrum, his Night-Gown and Breeches being torn in Pieces from his Body'. In October 1727 John Croucher stood in the 'Pillory in New Palace Yard, for Sodomitical Practices, and was very severely treated by the Populace' (*The British Journal*).

One of the most extreme displays of hostility came in 1810 against a group of men known as the Vere Street Coterie. Amos (alias Fox), James Cooke, Philip Ilett, William Thompson, Richard Francis, James Done, and Robert Aspinal were indicted for conspiring together at the White Swan, 'for the purpose of exciting each other to commit a detestable offence'. The events unfolded when a 'Molly House', the White Swan on Vere Street, which runs off Oxford Street, was raided by Bow Street police on Sunday 8 July 1810 and twenty-three people, described as being of a 'most detestable description' were arrested. Many of these customers were men from respectable society and of high rank who were more than happy to mix sexually with those of a lower class.

News of the raid spread quickly and very soon a mob of people began to congregate around Bow Street, where the accused had been taken. In total, twenty-seven men were arrested, but in the end the majority of them were released and only eight were tried and convicted. The men had to face the hostility of the crowd who kicked, punched and threw mud at them as they tried to leave the police station.

Over the course of the following week, six of the convicted men were found guilty of attempted sodomy and were pilloried in the Haymarket. Amos was sentenced to three years' imprisonment and to stand once in the pillory. Cooke, Ilett, Thompson, Francis and Done were each sentenced to two years' imprisonment and the pillory, and Aspinal was sentenced to one year's imprisonment.

The Times reported that the concourse of people that turned out 'was immense... even the tops of the houses in the Haymarket were covered with spectators'. It was estimated that there were about 40,000 people gathered. It was also a very violent and unruly crowd who had to come to vent their anger and were equipped with various objects to throw. The article noted that the women were particularly vicious. So large was the mob that the City had to provide a guard of 200 armed constables, half who were mounted and half on foot, to protect the men from even worse mistreatment.

The men were conveyed from Newgate to the Haymarket in an open cart. They all sat upright but could not help but look on in fear and dread as they saw the sight of the spectators on the tops of the houses hurling a cacophony of hisses and boos, accompanied by a volley of mud which made the men fall flat on their faces in the cart.

An old watch house near
the Old Bailey.

The mob formed a gauntlet along Ludgate Hill, Fleet Street, the Strand and Charing
Cross, and they lost no time in pelting the men with their assortment of projectiles.
By the time they arrived at the Haymarket at one o'clock in the afternoon, the pillory
would only accommodate four, so two men were taken to St Martin's Watch House to
wait their turn. Once a space was formed around the pillory, a number of women were
admitted to commence the proceedings. With great vigour they rained down a shower
of dead cats, rotten eggs, potatoes and buckets filled with blood, offal, and dung, which
had been brought by butchers' men from St James's Market. During the next hour
of agony the men walked constantly round the pillory, which was on a fixed axis and
swivelled.

The two remaining prisoners, Amos and Cooke, were then placed in the pillory, and
were also pelted till it was scarcely possible to recognize a human shape. The cart then
conveyed them through the Strand and to Newgate, the mob continuing to pelt them
all the way. By the time they reached Newgate some of them were cut in the head and
bled profusely.

The famous pillory at Charing Cross.

The Morning Chronicle blamed foreigners for such a crime committed by the prisoners:

> We avoid entering into the discussion of a crime so horrible to the nature of Englishmen, the
> prevalence of which we fear we must ascribe, among other calamities, to the unnecessary war
> in which we have been so long involved. It is not merely the favour which has been shown to
> foreigners, to foreign servants, to foreign troops, but the sending our own troops to associate
> with foreigners, that may truly be regarded as the source of the evil.

Two men, forty-two-year-old John Newbold Hepburn, formerly an officer in a West India regiment, and eighteen-year-old Thomas White, a drummer boy, were convicted of the act of sodomy despite not being present at the White Swan during the night of the raid. Both of them received the death sentence and were executed at Newgate on 7 March 1811.

7

Religious Sanctions

Before the Reformation and the break with the Roman Catholic Church in the 1530s, England had been for centuries a Catholic nation. However, there were many sects and individuals who challenged Church doctrine. Such views were considered heresy and heretics (those who challenge or propose change to an established system of belief) found themselves sentenced to death by burning.

The Burning of Lollards

At the end of the fourteenth century the Church came under attack from John Wycliffe (1324-1384), a Yorkshireman educated at Oxford. Wycliffe was one of the first recognised critics of the Church and his supporters, the Lollards, rejected the Roman Catholic Church, arguing that the Bible was the supreme authority, that the clergy should hold no property and that there was no basis for the doctrine of transubstantiation (the doctrine that the taking of bread and the wine changes into the substance of the body and blood of Christ during the Eucharist). The Lollards consisted mainly of itinerant preachers and Wycliffe wanted a reformation of the Church, arguing that it should give up all its worldly possessions.

Not surprisingly, the Lollards were vulnerable for advocating such dangerous ideas. Wycliffe was condemned as a heretic in 1380 and again in 1382. Fortunately for Wycliffe, he did not suffer the torments that were inflicted on many of his supporters as he died in 1384.

By the time of Henry IV's reign (1399-1413), the Crown and Church united against the Lollards and anti-heresy legislation was passed in 1382, 1401 and 1414, which gave legal authority to the burning of heretics. Execution by burning consisted of heaping faggots around a wooden stake, above which the prisoner was attached with chains or iron hoops. In the event of a small fire, the condemned would burn for a few minutes until death came from heat-stroke or loss of blood plasma. Victims might also die from suffocation.

The first Lollard Protestant martyr in England is thought to be William Sawtrey, who was burned at the stake in 1401 (although some accounts state that it was at Smithfield and others St Paul's Cross). Other Lollards followed and were executed in various places in London. John Badby, a tailor from Evesham, was convicted of heresy in 1410 after he refused to recant his beliefs.

The burning of Lollards at West Smithfield continued and included London merchants Richard Turming and John Claydon in 1415, and William Taylor, a priest, in 1423. John Claydon was accused of having seditious books in his house. William Taylor was accused of heresy but recanted and received absolution. Having gone through the ritual of forgiveness, Taylor pushed his luck and was caught a year later in 1419. After a long imprisonment, he was brought to Smithfield in March 1423, and burned at the stake.

Throughout the fifteenth and early sixteenth centuries, both secular and ecclesiastical authorities made efforts to stamp out the Lollards, although the repression became less intense. The Lollards became an underground movement and passed down their beliefs within families and through trade contacts. During the reigns of Henry VII (r.1485-1509) and Henry VIII (r.1509-1547), there were at least twelve Lollard trials, which included that of eighty-year-old Joan Broughton, the first woman to suffer martyrdom in England. Joan was burned at Smithfield in April 1494, along with her daughter.

By the sixteenth century West Smithfield had become increasingly populated with a maze of crowded lanes surrounding the area as well as large tenements, inns, brewhouses and pens for livestock ready for the market.

Throughout the reign of Henry VIII, Lollards and heretics continued to be burned. These included William Succling and John Bannister in October 1511 and John Stilincen in September 1518. Stilincen had previously recanted but was brought before Richard Fitz-James, Bishop of London, and condemned as a heretic. Amidst a vast crowd of spectators, he was chained to the stake and burned to death. James Brewster from Colchester followed him in 1519.

Carry On Executing

Henry VIII's break with the Roman Catholic Church in the 1530s began a process of religious change that led to the execution of both Protestant and Catholic martyrs. Elizabeth Barton, along with four of her promoters, was one of the first victims of the English Reformation. In April 1535, bishops were ordered to imprison clergy who continued to accept papal authority. The next month the cause célèbres of the age, the executions of London Carthusians Thomas More and John Fisher, took place.

The Carthusian monks Robert Lawrence, Augustine Webster, and Father John Houghton were executed at Tyburn. Maurice Chauncy, a Charterhouse monk, wrote that they were thrown down and fastened to a hurdle and were dragged at the heels of the horses through the city until they arrived at Tyburn. The journey from the prison was made over a road that was rough and hard in places, and wet and muddy in other parts.

When they came to the gallows, where many thousands had gathered, the executioner bent his knee before the condemned and asked forgiveness. The monks prayed before the ladder was moved away and then the rope was cut and the body of Houghton fell to the ground where it began to 'throb and breathe'. He was moved to an adjoining place where his garments were removed and he was laid naked on the hurdle. The executioner cut open his stomach and 'dragged out his bowels, his heart, and all else, and threw them into a fire'. His head was finally removed and his body was divided into quarters. The other monks followed and were subjected to their fate, 'all of their remains were thrown into cauldrons and parboiled, and afterwards put up in different places in the city'.

Other monks followed, such as William Exmew on 19 June 1535 along with Humphrey Middlemore, for being 'obstinately determined to suffer all extremities rather than to alter their opinion' with regard to the primacy of the Pope. They were made to stand in chains, bound to posts and were left in that position for thirteen days. They all suffered the sentence of being hanged and quartered.

A significant reaction to Henry's religious changes and the Dissolution of the Monasteries was the Pilgrimage of Grace, the name given to the religious rising in the north of England in 1536. Concerned by this event, Henry VIII responded decisively by executing the leaders as well as crushing the rising. In May 1537, two months after twelve Catholics had been brutally executed at Tyburn, Lord Darcy, Sir Henry Percy and several others involved in the Pilgrimage of Grace, together with the Abbots of Fountains, Jervaulx and Sawley, met a similar end.

The 1530s were a politically sensitive period and to speak out against Henry and his marriage to Anne Boleyn was treasonable. One particular victim of this legislation was Elizabeth Barton, a maidservant from Aldington in Kent known as the 'Holy Maid of Kent'. Since 1525 Elizabeth had suffered from a form of epilepsy which gave rise to trances. Consequently, she was credited with having some form of second sight. When Henry had divorced Catherine of Aragon in 1533, Elizabeth Barton was so outraged she prophesied that Henry would die within a month of his marriage to Anne Boleyn. This was considered to be more than a wild prediction and Elizabeth was arrested on grounds of treason. She was taken to the Tower and tortured, and the following year, in April 1534, she was condemned to hang at Tyburn. Barton was executed with Edward Bocking, John Dering and two monks from Canterbury, Richard Risby and Henry Gold. It is reputed that her head was the only one of a woman to be spiked and exhibited on the Drawbridge Gate of London Bridge. One of the first things that people would see as they came into London from Southwark over London Bridge was the Gatehouse, which was adorned by the spectacle of the heads of the executed, dipped in tar and displayed for all to see.

One high-profile execution was that of Bishop and Cardinal John Fisher (1469-1535). Fisher was executed by order of Henry for refusing to accept him as Head of the Church of England. He was beheaded on Tower Hill on 22 June 1535. His body was stripped and left on the scaffold till evening, when it was taken on pikes and

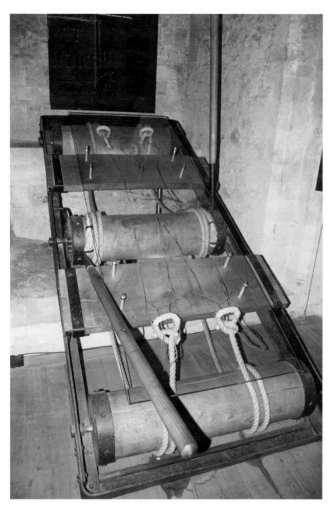

The rack.

thrown naked into a rough grave in the churchyard of All Hallows, Barking, although it was removed two weeks later and buried within the Tower of London. Fisher's head was stuck upon a pole on London Bridge, where it caused huge congestion on and around the bridge because of the numbers of people clamouring to see it.

Also in this decade, Richard Byfield was thrown into prison and whipped for supporting Protestant doctrines. Byfield was flogged on a number of occasions and eventually taken to the Lollard's Tower in Lambeth Palace where he was chained by the neck to the wall. In 1532 he was led to Smithfield to face the same fate as other heretics. John Forest, who had been a chaplain to Catherine of Aragon, was given the same treatment as poisonous cook Richard Rose in April 1538: he was sentenced to death at Smithfield where he was roasted alive for two hours in a cage over a log fire before he died. Another roasting came in 1542 when Margaret Davy was boiled to death for the crime of poisoning.

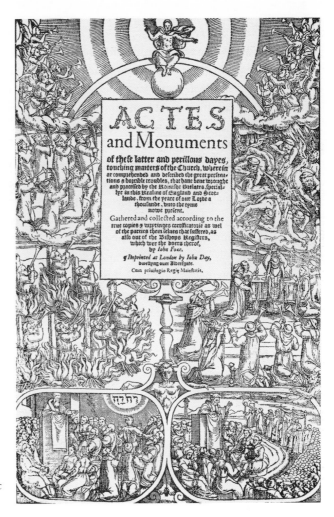

Title page of gory English classic
Foxe's Book of Martyrs.

For Protestants who read banned copies of William Tyndale's translation of the Bible the penalty was severe, as John Tewkesbury discovered. Tewkesbury was pinioned 'hand, foot, and head in the stocks' for six days without release. He was then whipped and had his eyebrows twisted with small ropes so that the blood spurted from his eyes. This was not the end, as he was then sent to the Tower and racked until he was nearly lame.

Similar agonies were meted out on Andrew Hewit and John Frith in 1533. Frith had come to England and distributed copies of Tyndale's Bible but was caught when the concealed books were found in his bag.

The fate of the unfortunate Anne Askew reflected the religious turmoil of the times. Anne, a Protestant, came to London where she was arrested for distributing leaflets. She was then subjected to such severe torture that she had to be carried to the stake at Smithfield; there she was burned in a chair with three other heretics.

The Marian Martyrs

More Protestants martyrs would find their place in John Foxe's eponymous classic during the reign of Catholic Queen Mary (1553-1558). Within two months of Mary becoming Queen, Protestants were being arrested on the flimsiest of charges. Many others fled abroad. In 1554 the medieval heresy laws were revived which led to the burning of 283 Protestant martyrs between February 1555 and November 1558 (including fifty-six women).

Burning at the stake during Mary's reign took on a particular significance. Persecutions began in January of 1555 when a number of eminent Protestants were subjected to hostile examination by a commission of leading bishops. Public executions were guaranteed to draw large crowds and the burning of the first Protestants under Mary was to be no exception. The first Protestant to be publicly burned at Smithfield in Mary's reign was John Rogers, Vicar of St Sepulchre's at Newgate. Rogers was asked to revoke his doctrines but refused, thus assuring his place as a martyr. On 4 February 1555 he was led the short distance from his prison to Smithfield through the large crowd. Among the mass of people who came to see the execution were his eleven children and his wife, who was holding their baby at her breast. Rogers was 'burnt

John Roger, Protestant martyr burned at Smithfield.

Memorial to the Marian Martyrs at Smithfield.

to ashes, washing his hands in the flame as he was burning'. Other martyrs who had appeared before the commission were executed elsewhere, many in the places where they had preached.

The martyrs came from diverse backgrounds and included butchers, barbers, drapers and weavers. One such weaver was Thomas Tomkins from Shoreditch who was burned at the stake at Smithfield in May 1555.

John Philpot, Archdeacon of Winchester, was taken to Smithfield at eight o'clock in the morning on 17 December 1555. When he arrived the ground was so muddy that two officers offered to carry him to the stake – an offer he declined. During the winter of 1555-56 more Protestants were arrested in London – John Tudson, Thomas Whittle, John Went, Thomas Brown, Isabel Foster, Joan Lushford and Bartlet Green. In January 1556 all seven were burned together at Smithfield. Three years into Mary's reign eighty-eight heretics had been burned, sixteen at Smithfield.

The burnings continued, and in April 1558 over forty men and women were arrested for attending a Protestant meeting in a field at Islington. Twenty were detained and sent to Newgate where they were promised a pardon on condition that they attended Mass.

By late 1558, at the age of forty-two, Queen Mary was dying at St James's Palace in Westminster. She requested to see Elizabeth in order to ask her to maintain the Catholic faith – but this was to be another lost cause. On 17 November 1558 Mary died and was succeeded by Elizabeth, much to the rejoicing of her Protestant subjects. Out of 283 Protestants burned during Mary's reign, seventy-eight had died in London and fifty-six at Smithfield.

Catholics at Tyburn

The reign of Elizabeth continued to witness religious persecutions – but this time it was mainly Catholics who would be executed and hailed as martyrs. Missionary and Jesuit Catholics who sought to convert people back to the faith found themselves condemned for treason. (The Elizabethan regime insisted that it executed Catholics as traitors and not for their religious opinions, whereas in Mary's reign Protestants had been executed as heretics.) Once identified as traitors, Catholics could be subjected to the dreaded penalty for treason: hanging and quartering. The English State, proud of its religious tolerance, demanded the execution of Catholics because they would not swear an oath accepting the Queen as Supreme Governor of the Church.

The infamous Tyburn gallows received many victims during the sixteenth century as a result of the religious changes that took place. For many Catholics, Mary, Queen of the Scots was seen as the stronger claimant to the throne and she became the focus for a number of plots which were intended to remove Elizabeth. The famous triangular gallows at Tyburn, the 'Triple Tree', was erected in 1571. It stood nearly 18ft high and prompted the poet John Taylor (1578-1653) to declare that 'Tyburn doth deserve before them all, The title and addition capital, Of Arch or great Grand Gallows of our Land, Whilst all the rest like ragged Lackeys stand'. The triangular frame of the gallows was capable of hanging eight people on each beam and up to twenty-four people at one time. It towered above the throngs of the assembled crowd. The road between Tyburn and the City (now Oxford Street) was particularly busy on execution days when it would have carried traffic going west to the gallows and also cattle going to Smithfield Market to the east.

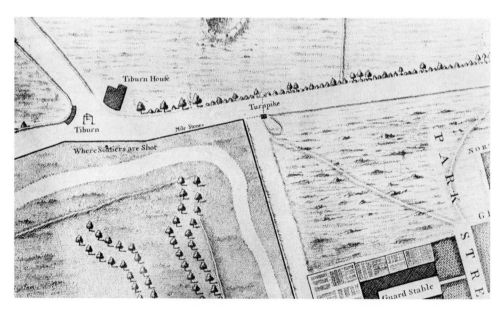

Tyburn gallows shown in Rocque's Map of London, 1746. The area is still rural.

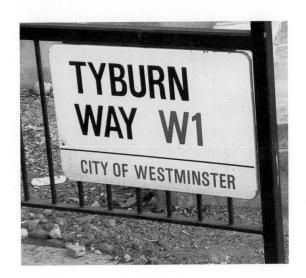

Tyburn Way, Marble Arch. Very few
reminders of Tyburn exist.

The first known execution on the triangular gallows was recorded on 1 June 1571: 'the saide [John] Story was drawn upon an herdell from the Tower of London unto Tiborn, where was prepared for him a newe payre of gallows made in triangular maner'. (*Harleian Misc.* iii. 1809: 100-8)

John Story was imprisoned in 1563 for his activities persecuting Protestants under Mary. Seven years later, after escaping, Story was captured and brought back to England. The crowd at the gallows was hostile and observers noted that 'he was the object of general execration and care was taken that he should suffer all the torments of that horrible sentence'. However, the prisoner managed to leave his mark: when the executioner was in the process of disembowelling him, Story summoned sufficient strength to raise himself up and aim a blow at his tormentor.

In many instances the executioner had some degree of discretion on how far he might inflict the punishment. He might decide whether or not to strangle the condemned before proceeding to the more barbaric aspects of disembowelling. However, there were many instances where the punishment of disembowelling was carried out without the mercy of death by hanging. Many more Catholic martyrs went to their death at Tyburn after John Story, including Thomas Woodhouse, a priest from Lincolnshire, John Nelson, Thomas Sherwood and Everard Hanse.

The gallows were considered to be a place of great spiritual and magical power, particularly in relation to martyrdom. For example, the hands of the executed were believed to possess curative powers, and there are many examples of people stroking themselves with a condemned man's hands after the execution. It was believed that the hangman was endowed with particular powers because of his relationship with the dead. Even touching the gallows brought certain dangers with it, and artisans who were involved with erecting the gallows had to go through a ritualised ceremony in order to be protected from the taint. The body of the condemned was thought by some to convey magical powers akin to the power of the King's touch – which was reputed to heal, and was synonymous with Jesus curing the ill by the touch of his hand.

A number of Catholics were executed at Tyburn in December 1581, most notably the Jesuit priest Edmund Campion. Campion and two other Catholic priests were dragged through the muddy streets to Tyburn where a large crowd was waiting. Campion sang all the way to his execution and even when he was cut down from the rope he stood upright and shouted, 'Lord, Lord, Lord' whilst struggling with the executioners.

In 1584 George Haydock, John Nutter, Thomas Hemerford, James Fenn and John Munden were accused of plotting against Elizabeth. They were drawn on hurdles with five other priests to Tyburn. The cart was then driven away, and the officer was said to have pulled the rope several times before Haydock fell. He was then disembowelled while alive. A similar fate awaited the other priests. One, James Fenn, a Somerset man about forty years of age and a widower with two children, was stripped of all his clothing with the exception of his shirt. After the cart was driven away his shirt was pulled off his back, so that he hung stark naked, 'whereat the people muttered greatly'.

Between 1581 and 1603, one hundred and eighty Catholics were executed for treason, most of these at Tyburn.

In 1595 the poet Robert Southwell was hanged at Tyburn. Southwell had ministered to Catholics and as a result was subjected to torture and three years' confinement in a dungeon before he was brought to trial and sentenced to the usual punishment of hanging and quartering. His torture had involved being hung from a wall by his hands, with a sharp circle of iron round his wrist pressing on his artery, his legs bent backwards and his heels tied to his thighs. When he arrived at Tyburn he was lifted on to a cart to be hanged. The hangman slowly strangled Southwell and when an officer began to cut the rope of the still breathing priest, Lord Mountjoy and other witnesses interrupted and told him to let Southwell alone to die. He was said to have inspired sympathy on the gallows, and some of the crowd appealed to the executioner to let him hang until he was dead.

The remains of a martyr's body were often rescued and, in some cases, saved for relics. For example Oliver Plunkett, Catholic primate of Ireland, was sentenced to death for plotting to aid a French invasion of Ireland in 1678. Plunkett was drawn through the City of London to Tyburn and hanged, drawn and quartered. His bowels were taken out and burnt before him, his head was cut off and his body divided into four quarters and disposed of. His head was rescued by friends and now remains preserved in the Catholic Church of St Peter's in Drogheda in the Irish Republic.

In the case of the Catholic Edmund Gennings at Tyburn, the executioner was requested to show the visitors pieces of flesh to satisfy their curiosity. In Genning's case the hangman, 'tooke up one of his [Gennings's] forequarters by the arme, which when he had shewed to the People, he contemptuosly flung it downe into the baskets agayne wherin it lay, and tooke up the head that they might see his face'.

Plaque to the Tyburn Martyrs, Tyburn Convent.

Tyburn Convent,
Bayswater Road.

There were occasions when the performance of the executioner drew theatre-like responses from the crowd. The crowd's sympathies might sway depending on the ways in which the condemned reacted to their punishment, or through the speeches. In 1601 after the priest Mark Barkworth had been quartered, it was noticed that constant kneeling had hardened his knees. Someone in the crowd picked up one of Barkworth's legs after the quartering and called out, 'Which of you Gospellers can show such a knee?'

The present Tyburn Convent on Bayswater Road, which was built in 1903, contains a number of relics including linen and straw stained with the blood of five Jesuit martyrs executed on 20 June 1679; bone from the finger of St John Roberts, hanged, drawn and quartered on 10 December 1610; fingernail of Thomas Holland, executed on 12 December 1642; sliced vertebrae of John Lockwood, executed 1642; and a bloody cloth from the robes of Oliver Plunkett.

A particular development in scaffold ritual from the sixteenth century was the last dying speech. Dying speeches were intended not only to demonstrate that crime did not pay but also to reinforce the desire for religious conformity during the Reformation. Gallows speeches were written and arranged in order that the condemned would proclaim their guilt, and intended as a warning to the crowds of the dangers of transgression and the need to uphold the virtues of the monarch and the State. The speech would vary from a plea for forgiveness to a claim of innocence or the opportunity to make a religious pronouncement. In many cases the speech involved a condemnation of the authorities. Some prisoners remained in silence while others were so drunk they rambled incoherently.

Anne Boleyn, the second wife of Henry VIII, said before her execution on 19 May 1536:

Good Christian people, I am come hither to die, for according to the law, and by the law I am judged to die, and therefore I will speak nothing against it. I am come hither to accuse no man, nor to speak anything of that, whereof I am accused and condemned to die, but I pray

Lincoln's Inn Fields, scene of the execution of the Babington Plotters.

God save the King and send him long to reign over you, for a gentler nor a more merciful prince was there never: and to me he was ever a good, a gentle and sovereign lord. And if any person will meddle of my cause, I require them to judge the best. And thus I take my leave of the world and of you all, and I heartily desire you all to pray for me. O Lord have mercy on me, to God I commend my soul.

At Lincoln's Inn Fields fourteen conspirators involved in the Babington Plot were hanged, drawn and quartered in 1587. Sir Anthony Babington, a zealous Roman Catholic, had hatched the plan, but he and his fellow plotters fell foul of Sir Francis Walsingham's spy network. Babington, as ringleader, was hanged first and had the misfortune still to be conscious when he had his penis cut off and was eviscerated. The discovery of this plot effectively sealed the fate of Mary, Queen of Scots, who was executed later in the same year at Fotheringhay Castle near Peterborough.

Witchcraft

The sixteenth century saw important developments in the persecution of 'witches'. From about the mid-fifteenth to the early eighteenth century, between 40,000 and 60,000 individuals were tried as witches and condemned to death in Europe. Of that number, as high as three-quarters of the victims were women. In England witchcraft persecutions really began in 1563 with the statute of Elizabeth I, but did not really become fully developed until the reign of James I (r.1603-1625). A further Witchcraft Act in 1604 broadened the penalty of death to anyone who invoked evil spirits or communed with familiar spirits.

Witches were hanged in England rather than burned, and were not subject to the same extremes of torture as in Europe (although elements of torture were not entirely absent). Nor were there mass executions in England such as those in France and Germany. Particular to English witchcraft trials were the ideas of 'pricking' to locate the Devil's mark, the use of 'possessed' children as accusers, counter-magic, demonic possession and the belief in so-called familiars (animals, domestic pets). After the Restoration in 1660 trials for witchcraft in England started to decline.

Middlesex and London did not have a Quarter Sessions and Assizes. Sessions of the Peace were held twice a year as well as Sessions of Inquiry. Hence those charged with witchcraft in Middlesex could be tried in the Session of Peace for Middlesex or Westminster, the Sessions of Gaol Delivery of prisoners from Newgate or the Old Bailey. After the Witchcraft Act of 1563, both Margaret Harckett (1585) and Anne Kerke (1599) were executed at Tyburn. After further revisions to the Act in 1604, Elizabeth Sawyer and Joan Peterson were executed in 1621 and 1652 respectively.

Sixty-year-old widow Margaret Harkett from Stanmore was the servant of William Goodwinne and her case is recorded in the contemporary pamphlet *The Severall factes of Witch-crafte*, where she is described as 'this ungodly woman... this witch'. She had been accused of a series of incidents which were said to have brought misfortune on a number of her neighbours. Margaret was arrested and brought before the justice for examination. She was then committed to Newgate where she remained until her trial and execution in 1585.

In 1599 Anne Kerke of Broken Wharf, London, was alleged to have disposed of a number of children by means of magic. Anne had attended the funeral of Anne Naylor, for whose mysterious death she had also been blamed. When Anne Kerke was offered no share in the traditional doles for the poor she was 'sorely vexed' and directed her magic against another member of the Naylor family. At her trial the justice tried to disprove the idea that a witch's hair could not be cut by taking ten or twelve hairs from her head. However, a sergeant who also attempted to cut the hairs with a pair of scissors claimed they had turned round in his hand, and the edges were so 'battered, turned and spoiled, that they would not cut anything'. Still determined, he attempted to burn the hair, but by all accounts the fire flew away from it.

The Witch of Edmonton was first performed in 1621 at the Cockpit in Drury Lane and took as its subject Elizabeth Sawyer. Elizabeth was brought to Newgate for causing the death of a neighbour by witchcraft. The court was unsure how to proceed with the evidence when a local JP, Arthur Robinson, intervened and told the court that Elizabeth had a mark upon her body and this would confirm the suspicion of witchcraft. The witch's mark, also called a Devil's mark, was 'proof' that an individual was a witch. On the advice of the JP the bench ordered officers to bring three women

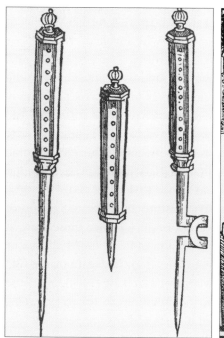

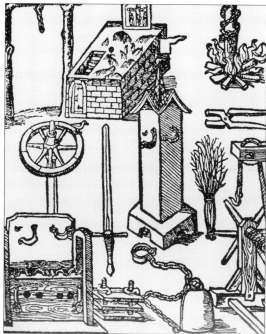

Implements for witch pricking.   The instruments of torture used on witches.

to do a body search of Elizabeth. The women claimed that they found a teat the length
and a half of a finger. This was considered sufficient evidence to condemn Elizabeth.

She did not confess easily. Her confirmation had to be extracted with great labour.
Her reluctance to confess would have further confirmed in the minds of many that
she fitted the pattern of a typical witch with her swearing, cursing and blaspheming.
Many Londoners, especially those who witnessed her execution, would have known
of Elizabeth's case because of the many accounts produced about her.

In 1652 Joan Peterson, the 'Wapping Witch', had been asked to act as an alibi in
what was a complex series of deceits involving the death of Lady Powell. Joan refused
to be involved and was subsequently arrested and had her house searched. Despite
a lack of evidence, she was subsequently charged with using witchcraft to kill Lady
Powell. Although she strongly denied the charge, claiming that she had never even
met Powell, she was also subjected to a search at her trial – and predictably was found
to have a 'teat' in her 'secret parts'. Many were bribed to testify against her and the
trial was clearly rigged. Joan continued to protest her innocence, though she was
offered a pardon if she would confess her crime. (During this particular offer Joan
responded by hitting one of the officers and making his nose bleed.) On 12 April
1652 Joan was brought to Tyburn. The minister pleaded with her to confess, to which
the executioner replied that 'he might be ashamed to trouble a dying woman'. Joan,
an innocent victim, was hanged.

Scold's Bridle

A scold's bridle was a torture device for women, resembling an iron muzzle or cage for the head with an iron curb projecting into the mouth and resting above the tongue. To add to the pain, the curb was often studded with spikes so as to torture the tongue if it dared move.

It was also used as corporal punishment for other offences, such as for female workhouse inmates. One is on display at the Tower of London. Another is at Walton-on-Thames, where it is displayed in the vestry of the church, dated 1633, with the inscription 'Chester presents Walton with a bridle to curb women's tongues that talk too idle'.

'The Bawdy Courts' – Church Courts

Alongside the criminal and civil courts and the courts of equity, there was a whole network of some 300 or 400 ecclesiastical courts whose activities affected many aspects of our ancestors' lives. Church courts existed from the Norman Conquest and ended in the mid-nineteenth century.

For centuries, the staple of Church court business were moral offences. These included slander, unseemly behaviour in church, working or rowdy drinking on a Sunday, neglect to have children baptised, simony, heresy, drunkenness, offences committed in the churchyard, witchcraft, usury, adultery, fornication, incest, blasphemy

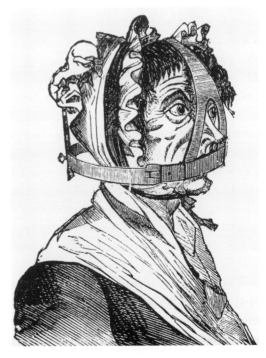

Scold's bridle.

and bastardy. The most common entry in Church court correction records relates to 'ante-nuptial fornication', which usually meant the wife was pregnant at marriage and that a child was born within six months of the wedding. The following charges were also commonly made: fornication between unmarried persons; indecent behaviour towards females; mutual male (and female) masturbation; coition with animals; communication of venereal diseases; lewd behaviour (which also included the singing of bawdy songs); keeping a brothel; being a whore; and incest.

It was the range of sexual offences that gave Church courts the more familiar nickname of 'the bawdy court'.

In *The Friar's Tale* Chaucer wrote about a fine Archdeacon who would boast, That Lechery was what he punished most…
And ere the Bishop caught them with his crook,
Down they went in the Archdeacon's book;
For he had Jurisdiction, after Detection,
And Power to Administer Correction.

All these offences were considered to be sins punishable by exclusion from church or by excommunication. These penalties could only be redeemed by penance (expressions of moral repentance), which the Church courts imposed on those found guilty. Penances involved some form of public confession and humiliation, such as standing in church in a white sheet or in sack-cloth, processing bare-foot or being publicly flogged. In many cases the accused was suspended from communion or church services. For pre-nuptial pregnancies the punishment was open confession in church. As for bigamy, which was not a civil offence before 1603, many couples ran away and married again. Buggery and bestiality carried the death penalty, and for having an illegitimate child the penalty was a hefty fine large enough to be financially ruinous for the majority of people. Before 1700 both mother and father were often stripped naked to the waist and whipped through the street at a cart's tail. It is hardly surprising that infanticide (an offence in 1624) was often resorted to by desperate mothers.

In 1559 the Act of Uniformity required people to attend church and failure to do so could incur a fine for recusancy – non-attendance. The business of the courts was conducted in Latin, which was incomprehensible to most Englishmen. Witnesses from all classes would be called upon to tell their story and invited to tell on their master or neighbour. The courts often proceeded on the basis of mere scandal and gossip, such as the Londoner who was reported in 1620 for wearing a dirty ruff at church and subsequently fined 54s.

Constables could haul suspects before a magistrate, as the constable Elbow in Shakespeare's *Measure for Measure* drags the bawd Pompey to justice on the suspicions of his wife. They even had the power to break into houses suspected of harbouring offenders. Minor officials, like the beadles or parish constables, spied out offences, often

Civil courts: the Royal Courts of Justice on the Strand.

at the prompting of neighbours. Neighbours did not need a great deal of prompting; they were happy to gossip about the most intimate details of family relationships and were quick to complain to the ecclesiastical courts of anything that violated local norms. London, as with other large cities, suffered less than smaller villages in rural areas.

Penance was often commuted for money, which worked to the advantage of the better off. The system was thus left open to corruption, which many judges were happy to exploit. Typically it was the poor that bore the brunt of punishments for all types of offences. In 1641 the publication *First and Large Petition of the City of London* argued that 'the prelates, corrupt administrators of justice' were responsible for 'the great increase and frequency of whoredoms and adulteries'. Also critical of the dispensing of justice was poet John Milton, who agreed with the publication by attacking 'the corrupt and venial discipline of clergy courts'.

The following cases, all from London, were punished with suspension from church services. In 1500 Thomas Hall 'of London' was charged for 'being a common breaker of faith and of the wicked crime of usury [charging of interest on loans]'. Nan Hoper committed perjury after contracting a marriage with Thomas Polard and then refusing to marry him. In 1476 Nicholas Haukyns was charged for not hearing divine service 'but lies in bed in the time of morning service Sunday after Sunday'.

The Spirituall Courts epitomized,
in a Dialogue betwixt two Proctors,
Busie Body, and Scrape-all, and their
discourse of the want of their
former imployment.

Runne Lamb.   Fly Duck.

Printed 1641.

Pamphlet showing a 'bawdy court' in 1641.

Christopher Kechyn was accused in 1496 of being 'a cheat and a seducer of many girls and an adulterer and dishonouring the sacrament of marriage with many women'. Nicholas Bembrick, a victualer of West Ham, refused to open his doors to the vicar and the churchwardens when they came to see why he was not attending service on Palm Sunday in 1615. In 1481, William Gyppe and his wife were required to purge themselves for being 'lewd persons'. In 1476, Thomas Ysakyr was suspended for showing 'his private parts to many women in the parish'. In 1482, William Clarke was suspended from church services for 'employing four foreigners'.

The case of John Gutton in 1489 might have been one for the secular courts to consider. He was ordered to pay 20s on four separate occasions 'for the use of Elizabeth Medigo with whom he committed adultery and whom he impregnated'. Peter Manyfield, a lewd and common procurer, 'carried away, by stealth against her will, a certain Alice Burle from her parents' house and kept her in his room for a long time, committing with her crimes of fornication'. In addition to his fine, Manyfield also received a temporary ban from church services.

Leticia Wall was given a penance in 1518 for not knowing the father of her child. She was made to 'precede the procession… with unconcealed face and bare feet and with a wax candle held up in her hand… and to say the psalm of the Blessed Mary during the mass'. In 1475, Joan Talbot had a child before marriage and was also ordered to precede the procession in her bare feet and a gown with a knotted kerchief covering her head.

Perjurer Robert Crouch avoided his punishment in 1500 for failing to pay 5s for a cloak: days before he was due to appear before the court, he died! The Church therefore had no option but to pray for his soul and discharge him. The punishment given to Francis Litton, 'a countryman', in 1632 is not specified but he was apprehended in St Paul's Cathedral for 'pissing against a pillar in the church'. In 1489, Lewis Ambrose committed adultery with Elizabeth Reynolds and had to pay a penance of 3s 4d. In Whitechapel in 1610 a group of women were standing inside the doorways of houses plying their trade when an Alice Rochester shouted to one of them, 'Thou art a whore and an arrant whore and a common carted whore and thou art my husband's whore'. Alice was sued for slander at the Church court. In November 1723, Lurana Knight was found guilty of fornication and was fined and whipped.

For not confessing during Lent or receiving the Holy Eucharist at Easter in 1491, Simon Paviour was suspended and excommunicated. Many parishioners were fined and punished for transgressing during Lent although many high churchmen continued to eat meat throughout this period as well as partake in other forbidden fruits. It was little wonder that the Church courts became increasingly unpopular. Churchmen were not always models of moral rectitude either. With the rise of an industrial and commercial economy, offences such as usury became more common; the old standards of perceived good conduct no longer applied. The courts themselves were known to be extortionate and corruptible on occasion. There was an eventual change in attitudes from the late seventeenth century, which saw a distinction between private sin and public law. Cases of sexual morality brought before Church courts in the eighteenth century declined dramatically as the shift towards a secular society continued.

8

Social Sanctions

Victorian institutions such as workhouses, hospitals, lunatic asylums and prisons were not intended to be places of joy. They inflicted punishments varying from the mild to the downright cruel and barbaric. In 1861 the census recorded 65,000 people in London institutions, approximately 37,000 males and 28,000 females.

The Workhouse

Our ancient system of poor relief dates from the sixteenth century, when parishes were made legally responsible for looking after their own poor. The funding for this came from the collection of a poor-rate tax from local property owners. However, by the start of the nineteenth century the cost of poor relief was increasing; at the same time, many believed that parish relief was an easy option for those who did not want to work. In 1834 the Poor Law Amendment Act was passed, which was intended to end all outdoor-relief for the able-bodied. Outdoor-relief was to be replaced by one of the most famous institutions of the past – the workhouse.

Around 15,000 parishes in England and Wales were formed into Poor Law Unions, each with its own union workhouse managed by a locally elected Board of Guardians. Hundreds of workhouses were erected across the country. This new Act used the threat of the Union workhouse as a deterrent to the able-bodied pauper. Poor relief would only be granted to those desperate enough to face entering the workhouse – and life inside the workhouse was intended to be as unpalatable as possible.

Food consisted of gruel – watery porridge – or bread and cheese, and inmates had to wear the rough workhouse uniform and sleep in communal dormitories. The able-bodied did work such as stone-breaking or picking apart old ropes called oakum. Workhouses consisted of the old, the infirm, the orphaned, unmarried mothers and the physically or mentally ill. In some cases it also included those who had been wealthy but had fallen on bad times. Entering the workhouse was considered the ultimate degradation.

OLIVER TWIST;

OR, THE

PARISH BOY'S PROGRESS.

BY "BOZ."

PLATES

DESIGNED AND ETCHED

BY GEORGE CRUIKSHANK.

LONDON:
RICHARD BENTLEY, NEW BURLINGTON STREET.
1838.

Oliver Twist famously asking for more food.

Describing a workhouse in 1838 in *Sketches in London*, James Grant commented:

Nothing but the direst necessity has compelled them to take refuge in these places: it is only when… they see absolute starvation staring them in the face, that such individuals have been induced to submit to the alternative of seeking an asylum in a workhouse. And once in, the idea of again coming out, until they are carried out in their coffins, never for a moment enters their mind. When they cross the gate of the workhouse, they look on themselves as having entered a great prison, from which death only will release them. The sentient creations of Dante's fancy saw inscribed over the gate of a nameless place the horrific inscription, 'All hope abandon, ye who enter here'.

The following is a summary of the rules drawn up for the conduct of the inmates at the workhouse in Hackney in the 1750s. Anyone not abiding by them could face imprisonment and be would be punished with the utmost rigour. Inmates were expected to observe the saying of prayers and to attend church. Anyone found loitering, begging, swearing or getting drunk was to be punished in the stocks. There was to be no distilled liquors brought into the house, and anyone causing a disturbance by brawling, quarrelling, fighting or using abusive language would lose one day's meal. For a second offence they would be put into the dark room for twenty-four hours. Inmates refusing to work were to be kept on bread and water, or expelled. Any person pretending to be sick in order to avoid work would appear before a magistrate. Inmates were also expected to clean themselves, wash and mend their clothes, and clean their dishes. Failure to do so meant having to suffer an appropriate punishment.

Institutions such as the workhouse often included sadists amongst the staff. *The Times* reported on 8 December 1868 that Mrs Wells, the matron of Bethnal Green Workhouse Schools at Leytonstone, came before the Board of Guardians on a charge of cruelty for ill-treating and beating girls placed under her care by the workhouse authorities. Her husband, the master, also had a charge against him for neglect and being drunk on duty.

At Hackney in 1894, Ella Gillespie, one of the school's nurses, was accused of 'systematic cruelty' to the children in her charge – allegedly beating them with stinging nettles and forcing them to kneel on wire netting that covered the hot water pipes. She also deprived them of water and made them drink from the toilet bowls. At night children would lay awake in fear, bracing themselves to face her 'basket drill'. Then they would be woken from their sleep and made to walk around the dormitory for an hour with a basket on their heads containing their day clothes, receiving a beating if they dropped anything. Gillespie was regularly drunk and in 1893 a local brewery supplied her with nineteen 4½ gallon casks of beer.

Other examples of her brutality included knocking the head of a thirteen-year-old girl against the wall seven times for talking to another girl. This incident happened as two girls were scrubbing the nursery floor, after a third girl entered and accidentally knocked over two scuttles of coal. Furious, Gillespie turned over four pails of water, and rubbed a girl's head into the wet coal on the floor. On another occasion she struck a girl with a bunch of keys, cutting her head and drawing blood. Many girls gave evidence against her, including thirteen-year-old Elizabeth Fawcett, who stated that Gillespie had slapped her face, pulled her hair and struck her with a frying pan. Alice Payne told how she and other girls were subjected to punishments such as laying naked on the bed whilst being thrashed with stinging-nettles. The evil and sadistic Gillespie was sentenced to five years' penal servitude.

In 1882 able-bodied men at Mary Place, Notting Hill, performed tasks such as stone-breaking, corn-grinding and oakum picking for fifty to sixty hours a week. The diet was basic and monotonous and smoking was forbidden. No inmate was ever allowed temporary leave from the premises.

The original St James's workhouse between Poland Street and Marshall Street in Soho was erected in 1725. During the eighteenth century this workhouse was reported to be in a 'very nasty condition, the stench hardly supportable, poor creatures almost naked and the living go to bed to the dead'. The workhouse was not without its own criminal activity, despite there being little worth stealing. For example, in October

Inside and outside of the Old Operating
Theatre, Southwark.

1818 fifty-six-year-old pauper Cuthbert Ramshaw stole a piece of woollen cloth worth 5s which was the property of the Governors and Directors of the Poor. For such ungrateful behaviour Ramshaw was whipped and given three months' confinement.

In 1818 seventeen-year-old John Dunn, who had spent his whole life as a pauper in the workhouse, stole one coat, a pair of trousers and a waistcoat belonging to James Horwood, master of the workhouse. Dunn, who was probably conditioned to the harshness of life in the institution, also received a whipping.

St Marylebone parish workhouse began operating in 1730. However, by the 1840s the demand for places in the workhouse exceeded 2,000 and with such high numbers there were pressures to economise. In 1856 allegations were made against workhouse staff for beating several young female inmates.

The punishment for being poor was severe enough, without any legal sanctions in addition. Even in death there was no escape, for the corpses of the impoverished were preyed upon by the body snatcher and the anatomist. The demand for corpses gave rise to the grisly activity of the resurrection men – the body snatchers. The only corpses available for medical study were those of hanged murderers. The 1832 Anatomy Act made it an offence to rob graves, so the only other corpses a doctor could legally dissect were the unclaimed bodies of people who had died in hospitals or workhouses. The stigma and fear of the workhouse was bad enough, but it was now made infinitely worse. Workhouses responded differently to the demands for the bodies of their poor. In the 1830s St Giles workhouse (average death rate of 200 per year) delivered 709 of its 'unclaimed' poor for dissection, while Marylebone gave up only fifty-eight. The system of delivering corpses of the poor also led to corruption. At St Giles parish in 1841, 'considerable excitement' was caused when it was discovered that the workhouse mortuary keeper, who had been bribed, decapitated a smallpox victim's body.

Social reformer Henrietta Barnett (1851-1936) played an important role in leading the movement to abolish the inhuman institutional care of pauper children and replace it with fostering. In her report, published in *The Cornhill Magazine*, there were 22,000 children in workhouses and 12,000 in the hateful barrack schools. Details of the care given in workhouses make shocking reading:

> The whole nursery has often been found under the charge of a person actually certified as of unsound mind, the bottles sour, the babies wet, cold and dirty… one feeble-minded woman was set to wash a baby; she did so in boiling water, and it died.

'Bedlam'

The most famous institution for the mentally ill was Bethlem Hospital, or 'Bedlam' (now known as the Bethlem Royal Hospital), based in Beckenham, south-east London. Although no longer in its original location, it is recognised as possibly the oldest psychiatric facility in Europe. The present hospital is at the forefront of psychiatric treatment, but for much of its history it was notorious for cruelty and inhumane treatment. Being mad was, in effect, a punishable condition.

The first site of Bedlam was in Bishopsgate Street in 1330. It became a hospital when the first Bethlem lunatics were recorded there in 1403. Conditions were awful and what care existed amounted to little more than restraining patients. Violent or dangerous inmates were manacled and chained to the floor or wall whilst some were allowed to leave and licensed to beg. By the late sixteenth century one inspection reported that there was great neglect, with the cesspit in dire need of emptying and the kitchen drains in need of replacing.

It was common practice in the eighteenth century for people to go to Bedlam to stare at the lunatics and even poke them with long sticks. There were some reforms, including the ending of casual public visiting in the 1770s; however, in 1814 the philanthropist Edward Wakefield was shocked when he encountered a patient:

A stout iron ring was riveted round his neck, from which a short chain passed through a ring made to slide upwards and downwards on an upright massive iron bar, more than six feet high, inserted into the wall. Round his body a strong iron bar about two inches wide was riveted;

Bedlam, as depicted by William Hogarth.

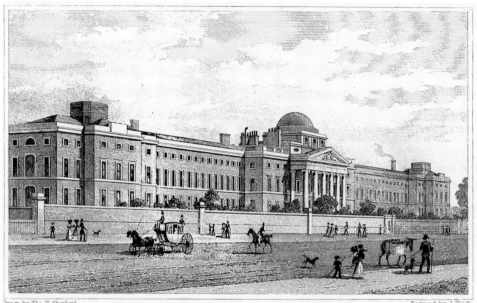

NEW BETHLEM HOSPITAL, ST. GEORGE'S FIELDS.

Bethlem Hospital in 1828.

on each side of the bar was a circular projection; which being fashioned to and enclosing each of his arms, pinioned them close to his sides.

One patient, James Norris, had suffered this type of treatment for twelve years. Wakefield's disclosure led to the setting up of a Parliamentary committee to investigate asylums, which in turn revealed some shocking evidence. Here is Wakefield's description of the women's galleries:

> One of the side rooms contained about ten patients, each chained by one arm or leg to the wall, the chain allowing them merely to stand up by the bench or form fixed to the wall, or to sit down on it. The nakedness of each patient was covered by a blanket-gown only.

Mercifully, the findings at least led to a new start when rebuilding began, including the addition of blocks for criminal lunatics.

However, in 1851 there was a scandal over the death of a patient which led to a further inquiry. This again exposed a number of unpleasant cases of ill-treatment. For example, the case of patient Hannah Hyson typified the worst sort of cruelty and wanton neglect. Her father wrote to the president of Bethlem, Sir Peter Laurie, complaining of his daughter's treatment. He noted over twenty wounds and lacerations on her body and described how her bones were almost showing through her skin. Tragically, Hannah died shortly after the letter was written.

Hannah's case was soon followed by that of Ann Morley who complained she had been hit by a nurse, forced to sleep on straw in the basement and hosed down with cold water despite being ill. Anne's complaints opened the door for other patients who told of their experiences. Some of these were in a skeletal condition, whilst others told of being force fed (which led in at least one case to a man dying).

In 1815 Bethlem was moved to St George's Fields, Southwark – now the site of the Imperial War Museum – and in 1930 the hospital was moved to the site of Monks Orchard House, Beckenham.

Schools

The most commonly experienced sanction is undoubtedly school punishment. Parliament abolished corporal punishment in state schools in 1986, though the verbal reprimand and the feared detention remain (a staple of school punishment for years). Gone are the days when a good thrashing would be meted out for almost any misdemeanour, or when pupils had to stand on a stool at the back of the class wearing a tall, cone-shaped hat decorated with a large 'D' for dunce.

At the beginning of the nineteenth century, children were not required to go to school but, by 1899, all children up to the age of twelve officially had the opportunity of going to school. Education depended on how wealthy families were. Rich children could be educated at home by a private tutor or governess; boys were sent to boarding schools such as Eton or Harrow. The sons of middle-class families attended grammar schools or private academies. The only schools available for poor children were charity and Church schools or 'dame' schools set up by unqualified teachers in their own homes. Ragged schools were introduced in the 1840s.

In 1854 Reformatory Schools were set up for offenders under sixteen years old. These were very tough places, with stiff discipline enforced by frequent beatings. Young people were sent there for long sentences – usually several years. The schools provided industrial training for juvenile offenders. In 1886 John Tarry appeared before the Old Bailey for assaulting a thirteen year-old girl. His punishment was seven days' imprisonment, eight strokes with a birch rod and two years in a reformatory school.

Punishment in the Workplace

The extent and regularity of severe and brutal punishment in workplaces, particularly small workshops that employed young children, cannot be exaggerated.

In 1685 Ann Hollis from the City of London was indicted for killing her apprentice, fourteen-year-old Elizabeth Preswick, with a rod of birch. Hollis took the girl upstairs and, with the help of two other girls, held Elizabeth on the bed whilst she whipped

The Old Bailey from the Viaduct public house.

her on the 'back, belly, shoulders and legs' so much that she passed out. Elizabeth died shortly after. Hollis said that she only whipped her a few times for 'lying' and 'being lazy'. Elizabeth was a 'sickly girl' who, it was concluded, had died of a consumption. Clearly this proved to be a fortunate decision for Hollis, who was acquitted.

A particularly evil employer was the infamous Sarah Metyard and her daughter, Sarah Morgan Metyard. Metyard senior employed young girls from parish workhouses to work as milliners. In 1758, thirteen-year-old Anne Naylor was subjected to dreadful cruelty. Anne and her sister were apprenticed as milliners to Sarah Metyard along with five other young girls (all of whom had come from workhouses). Anne was described as being of 'a sickly disposition' and therefore found the work difficult; she could not keep up with the other girls. This singled her out and made her the object of the fury of the Metyards. They punished Anne with such barbarity and repeated acts of cruelty that she decided to flee. Unfortunately, however, she did not get far: she was brought back, confined in an upstairs room and fed with little more than bread and water. For such a sickly child this could only weaken her further. Nonetheless, she seized another chance to escape – but was again returned. Poor Anne was thrown back into her prison, where she awaited the fury of the Metyards. As the old woman held her down the daughter began to beat Anne savagely with a broom handle. They then tied her hands behind her and fastened her to door, where she remained for three days without food or water. The other apprentices were not allowed to go anywhere near the room on pain of punishment. Alone, bruised, exhausted and starved, her speech failed her. By the fourth day she was dead.

Despite the dire warnings, some of the other girls saw her body tied with cord and hanging from the door. They cried out to the sadistic women to help Anne. The daughter ran upstairs and proceeded to hit the dead girl with a shoe. It was apparent that there was no sign of life and pathetic attempts were made at reviving her. One of the young apprentices, Philadelphia Dowley, acted as a witness four years later at the trial of the Metyards at the Old Bailey (July 1762). When asked why Anne tried to run away she replied, 'because she was… so ill. She used to be beat with a walking stick and hearth brooms by the mother, and go without her victuals'. Another witness, Richard Rooker, had been a lodger at Metyard's house. He told of the grisly attempt to conceal the crime, the revelation of other murders and how Metyard's daughter had told him with great reluctance what happened. There was a reluctance to announce the death and bury Anne as it would be clear from the state of her body that she had starved to death. Instead, Anne's body was carried upstairs into the garret and locked up in a box, where it was kept for upwards of two months until it 'putrefied, and maggots came from her'. The Metyards cut the body into pieces and then burned one of the hands in a fire. They then proceeded to dump the remains of the body near Charterhouse Street. The remains were discovered by a nightwatchman, who reported it to the 'constable of the night'.

Four years had passed since Anne's murder and it seemed that she would be denied justice. However, the continual arguments between Metyard senior and her daughter

Cock Lane, near to where Anne Naylor's remains were dumped.

resulted in frequent beatings for young Sarah Metyard, who wrote a letter to the overseers of Tottenham parish informing them about the whole affair and exposing her mother as a murderer. Both mother and daughter were subsequently arrested and indicted for the wilful murder of Anne and her eight-year-old sister, Mary Naylor. Both mother and daughter were executed at Tyburn and then taken to the Surgeon's Hall for dissection.

Another notorious case of physical abuse of servants in the eighteenth century concerned one Elizabeth Brownrigg. Yet again the unfortunate victims were orphaned young girls. Elizabeth Brownrigg was married to James Brownrigg, a plumber who, after spending seven years in Greenwich, came to London and took a house in Flower-de-Luce Court, Fleet Street. Elizabeth, a midwife, was appointed to look after women in the poorhouse run by the parish of St Dunstan-in-the-West. On one particular occasion, she had received three apprentices who she took into her own house where they did domestic service in order to learn a trade. Mary Mitchell was one of the apprentices appointed in 1765, and Mary Jones from the Foundling Hospital soon followed her. Jones quickly fell victim to Brownrigg's own brand of punishment: she was made to lie across two chairs in the kitchen while Brownrigg whipped her with such ferocity that she was 'obliged to desist through mere weariness'. Brownrigg would then throw water on her victim and often thrust her head into a pail of water. Poor Mary Jones had no one she could turn to. Her suffering was unimaginable.

Eventually she managed to escape, and found her way back to the Foundling Hospital where she told of her beatings. A surgeon examined her and found her wounds to be of a 'most alarming nature'. A solicitor wrote on behalf of the governors to Elizabeth Brownrigg's husband, James, threatening prosecution. Typically, the letter was completely ignored and the governors did not follow up the case. Unfortunately Mary Mitchell, who was still in the service of Brownrigg, was subjected to similar cruelty over the period of a year. She too managed to escape – but ran into the younger son of the Brownrigg's (they had sixteen children) during her flight and she was forced back into the house where her suffering intensified.

Tragically another girl with an infirmity, Mary Clifford, joined the Brownrigg household. She was frequently tied up naked and beaten with a hearth broom, a horsewhip or a cane. In addition, she was made to sleep in a coal cellar and was almost starved to death. She became so desperate with hunger that she broke into a cupboard for food – and paid a terrible price. For a whole day she was repeatedly beaten with the butt-end of a whip. A jack-chain was put around her neck and tied to the yard door: it was pulled as tight as possible without actually strangling the girl.

Another sadistic punishment that Brownrigg inflicted on the girls was to tie them to a hook in the timber beam and horsewhip them. Eventually Mary Clifford told of her treatment to a French lady who was staying in the house. When the woman confronted Brownrigg with this, she flew at Mary Clifford with a pair of scissors and cut her tongue in two places. Finally, when Mary Clifford's stepmother went to visit her on

The sadistic Elizabeth Brownrigg flogging a servant girl.

12 July 1767, the tyranny of the Brownriggs came to an end. The stepmother was refused entry by one of the servants, who had been instructed to deny that the girl was there. The stepmother was not satisfied and persuaded Brownrigg's next-door neighbour to post one of his servants, William Clipson, to watch the Brownrigg's house and yard. Clipson saw a badly beaten and half-starved girl in the yard and reported it to the overseer of St Dunstan's, who went to the house and demanded that the Brownriggs produce Mary, which they did after an altercation. Mary Clifford was eventually found locked in a cupboard. Her stepmother described her as being in:

> a sad condition, her face was swelled as big as two, her mouth was so swelled she could not shut it, and she was cut all under her throat, as if it had been with a cane, she could not speak; all her shoulders had sores all in one, she had two bits of rags upon them.

After much suffering over too long a period, the parish authorities finally took some action: James Brownrigg was arrested, although his wife and elder son escaped with a gold watch and a purse of money. Both Mary Jones and Mary Clifford were taken to St Bartholomew's Hospital where Mary Clifford died a few days later. A landlord

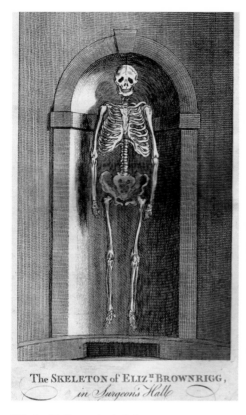

The SKELETON of ELIZ.ᵗ BROWNRIGG, in Surgeon's Hall

Elizabeth's Browning's skeleton.

Anatomy Theatre, Surgeon's Hall.

later informed on Elizabeth Brownrigg and her son, and they were duly arrested and kept in Newgate Prison. In her defence Brownrigg stated that, 'I did give her several lashes, but with no design of killing her; the fall of the saucepan with the handle against her neck, occasioned her face and neck to swell; I poulticed her neck three times, and bathed the place, and put three plaisters to her shoulders'. However, Mr Young, the surgeon, disputed that Mary's neck injury could have been caused by a saucepan handle.

When Brownrigg went to Tyburn to be executed the mob were outraged and vented their anger by pelting her with anything they could get their hands on. After her execution her body was cut down and taken to Surgeon's Hall where, after dissection, it was hung for people to see.

Elizabeth Wigenton of Ratcliff was hanged in September 1681 for a similar murder. Wigenton, a coat maker, had taken thirteen-year-old Elizabeth Houlton as an apprentice. One day Wigenton fetched one John Sadler to hold the girl, who was tied up and flogged with 'a bundle of rods so unmercifully, that the blood ran down like rain till the girl fainted away and died soon after'. Both Wigenton and Sadler were convicted of the murder and condemned to hang.

Caning apprentices was not uncommon. In the absence of a universal educational system, prior to the nineteenth century apprenticeships were the ways in which young boys acquired a craft. Many apprentices came into London from elsewhere and were often introduced to a harsh regime. It was not surprising that there was a high drop-out rate. In the London Livery Co., an apprentice was subject to the company's discipline, as well as to the daily supervision of his master; offences against his master were punished by whippings administered in the company hall. In 1630 the Spectacle Makers' Ordinances stated that:

> ...if any Apprentice shall misbehave himself towards his Master or Mistress... Or be any Drunkard haunter of Taverns, Ale Houses, Bowling Alleys or other lewd and suspected Places of evil Company... he shall be brought to the Hall of the said Company... and there these or such like notorious faults justly proved against him before the Court of Assistants... (he) shall be stripped from the middle upwards and there be whipped...

The practice continued centuries later. In 1848 John Harding was indicted at the Old Bailey for cutting and wounding his apprentice, Edward Jobling, who said that Harding had grabbed him by the collar and struck him many times with a cane. Jobling said that 'he beat me a great deal of good, I felt the blood immediately he had caned me; I felt it with my hand, looked at it about five minutes after – when he went up stairs, I undid my clothes, and saw the blood'.

Karl Marx (1818-1883) saw the cruelty and exploitation in the system of parish workhouses farming children out to work, often to cruel employers. He wrote that:

> The small and nimble fingers of little children being by very far the most in request, the custom instantly sprang up of procuring apprentices from the different parish workhouses of London... Many, many thousands of these little, hapless creatures were sent down into the north, being from the age of 7 to the age of 13 or 14 years old. The custom was for the master to clothe his apprentices and to feed and lodge them in an 'apprentice house' near the factor... Cruelty was, of course, the consequence... they were flogged, fettered and tortured in the most exquisite refinement of cruelty... they were in many cases starved to the bone while flogged to their work and... even in some instances... were driven to commit suicide.

9

Pleasurable Punishments

Seeking punishment for pleasure has a long history. Brothels catered for every perversion and kept a ready stock of instruments such as rods, whips and even more sophisticated devices. In the late eighteenth century flagellation was advertised and sought after, particularly by those who could afford the more expensive treatment. In Bloomsbury, Mary Wilson promoted her practice and women through the publication *The Exhibition of Female Flagellants*, boasting the best whippers in town. In Covent Garden, Mrs Collett's establishment was frequented, not surprisingly, by the Prince Regent.

The nineteenth century witnessed a proliferation of literature relating to flagellation, such as *The Exhibition of Female Flagellants* (1860), *The New Ladies' Tickler* (1866), *Romance of Chastisement* by George Stock (1870), and its sequel the *Quintessence of Birch Discipline* (1883), *With Rod and Bum, Or Sport in the West End of London* by Ophelia Cox (1898) and *Lady Bumtickler's Revels* (1872).

Theresa Berkeley was a well-known dominatrix and a brothel owner in the West End during the mid-nineteenth century. She ran brothels first in Soho and then in Charlotte Street. Her specialty was flagellation and she was notable as the inventor of the 'Berkeley Horse', a notorious machine used to flog gentlemen. Henry Spencer Ashbee (1834-1900), a book collector of pornography, described her repertoire:

Her instruments of torture were more numerous than those of any other governess. Her supply of birch was extensive, and kept in water, so that it was always green and pliant: she had shafts with a dozen whip thongs on each of them; a dozen different sizes of cat-o'-nine-tails, some with needle points worked into them; various kinds of thin bending canes; leather straps like coach traces; battledoors, made of thick sole-leather, with inch nails run through to docket, and currycomb tough hides rendered callous by many years flagellation. Holly brushes, furze brushes; a prickly evergreen, called butcher's bush; and during the summer, a glass and China vases, filled with a constant supply of green nettles, with which she often restored the dead to life. Thus, at her shop, whoever went with plenty of money, could be birched, whipped, fustigated, scourged, needle-pricked, half-hung, holly-brushed, furze-brushed, butcher-brushed,

'Pleasures of the Whip' by Aubrey
Beardsley.

stinging-nettled, curry-combed, phlebotomized [act of opening a vein by incision or puncture
to remove blood as a therapeutic treatment], and tortured till he had a belly full.

Theresa's instruments of pleasure were much sought after by the aristocracy and the
rich. In her famous Soho brothel the reception rooms were garishly decorated. In one
of the rooms, the 'Skeleton Room', a skeleton could be made to step out of a closet
with the aid of machinery. Henry Mayhew described some of the bizarre rooms and
her elaborate theatrical sets:

…rooms were fitted with springs, traps and other contrivances, so as to present no appearance
other than an ordinary room, until the machinery was set in motion. In one room, in which
a wretched girl might be introduced, on her drawing a curtain as she would be desired, a
skeleton, grinning horribly, was precipitated forward, and caught the terrified creature, in his,

to all appearances, bony arms. In another chamber the lights grew dim, and then seemed to gradually to go out. In a little time some candles, apparently self-ingnited, revealed to a horror stricken woman, a black coffin, on the lid of which might be seen, in brass letters, ANNE, or whatever name it had ascertained the poor wretch was known by. A sofa, in another part of the mansion, was made to descend into some place of utter darkness; or, it was alleged, into a room which was a store of soot or ashes.

Berkeley also enjoyed having a certain amount of torture inflicted on her by her clients – for the right price. She employed women who were prepared to take any number of lashes provided the flogger forked out enough.

The West End was well placed to provide brothels for rich patrons who would happily pay for the additional erotic and painful pleasures. Henry Spencer Ashbee wrote that very sumptuously fitted-up establishments, exclusively devoted to the administration of the birch, were not uncommon in London... It would be easy to form a very lengthy list of these female flagellants, but I shall restrict myself to mention a few only. Mrs. Collett was a noted whipper, and George IV is known to have visited her; she had an establishment in Tavistock Court, Covent Garden, whence she removed to the neighbourhood of Portland Place... Then came Mrs. James, who had... a house at No. 7 Carlisle Street, Soho. There were also Mrs. Emma Lee, real name Richardson, of No. 50 Margaret Street, Regent Street... But the queen of her profession was undoubtedly Mrs. Theresa Berkley... she was a perfect mistress of her art, understood how to satisfy her clients, and was, moreover, a thorough woman of business, for she amassed during her career a considerable sum of money. When she died in September 1836 she had made ten thousand pounds during the years she had been a governess.

Whipping was a common punishment and meted out to offenders irrespective of age and gender. For example, in 1679 four eight year-old boys were tried for stealing forty-eight bottles of ale from Francis Wheeler in St Martins. All of them confessed and were immediately taken out of the court and whipped. Likewise, twelve year-old Susanna Saunders was found guilty of stealing a hood and a pair of laced ruffles in 1684, for which she was publicly whipped. However, there was a thin line between those who meted out whippings as a genuine punishment and the secret pleasure some floggers derived from it. Such practices were all too common in certain institutions. In 1907 two sixteen-year-old boys, John Courtman and Albert Ingleton, who appeared at the Old Bailey for stealing a bicycle, were considered to be 'too old to be flogged' and were each given a four-month prison sentence.

The Revd Wm. M. Cooper wrote in a nineteenth-century standard work on corporal punishment (*A History of the Rod in all Countries from the Earliest Period to the Present Time*, London, William Reeves, 1877). In 1858 special regulations were issued for the punishment of naval cadets. They were not to be flogged according to the Mutiny Act, but simply with a birch rod, such as is used in public schools. Four cadets of the *Illustrious* having been guilty of such gross misconduct as would justify their dismissal from the service, the admiral in command suggested that they should be flogged with a birch rod… and the Admiralty sanctioned that course. In the circular issued from Whitehall to all commanders-in-chief, captains, and other commanding officers, it was enjoined that boys should not be flogged as formerly with a cat, but that in all cases where the offences could not be lightly passed over they should be punished in a similar manner to that which is in use at our large public schools – viz., by birching – and that in no case should more than twenty-four cuts be inflicted.

Birching had long been a standard punishment for boys, especially at the Royal Hospital School in Greenwich. Coldbath Fields Prison in Clerkenwell had until 1850 housed men, women and children; thereafter it was restricted to adult male offenders over the age of seventeen. Despite its aspirations to be a more humanitarian prison (it was designed by reformer John Howard), it became notorious for its strict regime of silence and its use of the treadmill. A cat o' nine tails had been used on boys where Sergeant Adams the warden spoke of its effectiveness when he compared it to the birch. Acting as a witness for the Report of the Reformatory Schools Committee, 1856 he noted:

> The punishment of flogging boys with the cat-o-nine-tails ought to be abolished not only as being too cruel but as being one which boys do not care about. We have substituted at Middlesex whipping with a birch rod, and boys who laugh at being put into a dungeon, and doubly laugh at flogging with a cat-o-nine-tails are upon their knees blubbering and praying not to be flogged with a birch rod – it deters them more than anything. I often sentence a boy given a month's imprisonment to be well birched at the end of the first fortnight, so as to keep the terror over his mind.

Boys were birched during the daily exercise hour at Coldbath Fields. On some occasions it was so severe that that their yells could be heard through the window of a punishment cell on one of the top floors.

10

Changing Attitudes

Debates over deterrence, retribution and appropriate punishments for criminal acts have continued unabated over the centuries. Today we would recognize the issues that plagued earlier generations: a perception that crime is increasing, the law is too soft, prisons are overcrowded and punishments are not severe enough. Reformers argued about the purpose of punishment. Was it about making the criminal pay or reforming them, or both?

Before the nineteenth century people had gathered in their thousands around the scaffold or pillory to either vent their anger towards the condemned or to watch with discernment or sympathy. Public displays of barbarous torture, pain and death were the largest of all attended events. The whole ritual surrounding the execution – the procession to the gallows; selling of food, drink and broadsheets; opportunities for pickpockets; drunken revelry and fights; the last dying speech followed by the agonising death throes of the condemned; the undignified scramble for the dead body by agents of the anatomists and the family of the deceased – were all part of the performance. Public executions were a regular feature of London life. All this took part against a background of no organized police force, and when prisons functioned as holding places until the accused were punished.

Henry Grattan (1746-1820), MP and campaigner for legislative reform, wrote, 'The more you hang, the more you transport, the more you inflame, disturb, and disaffect'. Henry Fielding (1707-1754), writer and legal reformer, also pointed out the disregard that many showed towards the scaffold. Commenting on the execution of eleven felons at Tyburn, he said, 'In real truth, the executions of criminals, as at present conducted, serve, I apprehend, a purpose diametrically opposite to that for which they were designed; and tend rather to inspire the vulgar with a contempt of the gallows rather than a fear of it'.

For many critics, the regular displays of violence in the pillory, whippings or public executions only hardened the attitudes of onlookers. Frequent exposure would 'harden the heart' wrote one commentator in 1773. Others asked whether repeated viewings

The ritual of being drawn to the place of execution.

Dr Cameron drawn on a Sledge to Tuburn

of such violence would make a person 'become indifferent to the spectacle'. The
Gentleman's Magazine in 1784 wrote that 'those who attend hangings go with the same
ease and indifference they would go to a race'. Charles Dickens, who attended the
execution of Francois Courvoisier, the valet who murdered Lord William Russell, wrote
of the crowd, '…no sorrow, so salutary terror, no observance, no seriousness; nothing but
ribaldry, debauchery, levity, drunkenness, and flaunting vice in fifty other shapes'.

Between the Restoration in 1660 and the mid-nineteenth century, there were
significant changes in criminal law, in the reform of prisons and in punishments.
The introduction of lawyers as prosecuting and defence counsel was a significant
development. But it was in the system of punishments that the biggest changes were
seen. As the population of London grew and the metropolis expanded, levels of crime
increased in response. The number of acts that carried the death penalty, the 'Bloody
Code', was in excess of 200 by the turn of the nineteenth century. New methods of

Scotland Yard, Whitehall. New forces in fighting crime.

Blue lamp indicating the Metropolitan Police Force.

punishment were introduced, such as the hulks and transportation. In the nineteenth century new prisons with the purpose of incarnating criminals were built, such as Pentonville and Millbank and after 1829 the Metropolitan Police force was established. From 1830 the number of capital offences had diminished and the last public execution took pace in 1868 outside Newgate Prison.

Institutional punishments continued, although greater checks on abuses, especially against young children, were put in place. The death penalty for murder was effectively ended under the Murder (Abolition of the Death Penalty) Act in 1965. In 1998 under Section 36 of the Crime and Disorder Act the last two offences carrying the death penalty in the UK – piracy with violence and treason – were finally abolished. This brought an end to a practice that had existed as a common punishment in Britain for over 1,000 years.